SO YOU WANNA BE A NEW YORK ACTOR?

A Guidebook to Creating a Fulfilling Career...
While Paying the Rent

By Josselyne Herman-Saccio and Guy Olivieri

TABLE OF CONTENTS

Introduction

HOW THIS BOOK CAME TO BE

"Go confidently in the direction of your dreams. Live the life you have imagined."
— **Henry David Thoreau**

The Personal Manager:

True Story from Josselyne

I have been managing actor's careers for a dozen years. Occasionally I find clients who are not only talented as performers but also great at marketing themselves. Guy Olivieri is by far the most incredible self-marketer I have ever met. I have represented him for more than five years, and when he came to me he had little-to-nothing on his resume and was a member of no unions, but he was a talented actor/singer and incredibly likable. We started working together, and, step-by-step, his career has been building since that day. He is organized, smart and professional. As more and more success came his way I kept saying, "I wish all my clients were like you, Guy" (half joking—but only half).

He started to develop a coaching business called Actors Who Make Money, coaching actors on how to market themselves and how to pursue acting while being able to pay the rent. At about the time we started talking about him writing a book, I had started writing a guide for actors on how to have a fulfilling career whether they were working or not. In an "Aha!" moment, we decided to collaborate and create a guide for actors on how to not only have a fulfilling career, but also pay the bills. Hence this book was born.

The Actor:

True Story from Guy

There is so much luck involved in an actor's career. Even the most talented actors can remain undiscovered for years, just because they were never in the right place at the right time. Being at luck's mercy is what makes actors' lives so frustrating. What can you do to minimize luck's effect on your career?

Over five years ago, at the suggestion of a friend, I did my first headshot mailing: I collected every single name and address I could find, I wrote a snappy cover letter and attached it to my shoddy picture and pretty-much empty resume, and I mailed it all out. Two hundred and seventeen envelopes: I still remember that.

I got maybe six calls based on that mailing and, very luckily, one was from Joss. It was a great bit of luck that she saw something valuable in my sad envelope. She auditioned the hell out me: monologues, songs, and interviews, and we decided to start working together. And "working together" is the proper term.

Now, I had someone to help me. I had someone to increase my opportunities, and someone to guide me in the right direction. The luck factor was shrinking.

It was at that point that I decided I was going to take that "luck factor" and start stamping it into the ground. This book is about controlling every aspect of your career that is controllable, through powerful marketing and through a personal philosophy about how to live your life as an artist.

Luck will always be a factor. But when you have luck beat down to the tiniest possible size, when you're controlling everything you can control, you'll be amazed how much your life will change. When you know you're doing everything within your power to make your career happen, you simply relax. You live your life, as an actor and as a human being, with much less anxiety.

And you will see results. I certainly have! In the last five years, I've joined all three unions, I've done national tours, shot dozens of commercials, acted in a ton of films and on television, and I've made enough money in showbiz that I don't have to have another job to survive. Sound appealing? Keep reading.

YOUR DREAMSOURCE

This book will detail a combination of ways to create fulfillment in your career through what we call your DreamSource, as well as the step-by-step process of obtaining success in that career.

Your DreamSource is the **underlying motivation for why you are an actor in the first place.** What is the ultimate driving force behind your desire to succeed in the entertainment business? Discovering your DreamSource is ultimately the secret to having a fulfilling career, whether you are working as an actor or not.

Unless you bring your DreamSource to your work (and your life) right now, versus trying to *get* something from your career, you may never really be fulfilled—except for brief moments here and there. The very nature of the existing paradigm in which most actors work is designed to keep them reaching for the next, bigger, shinier object (see Chapter Six, "The Next Carrot Syndrome"), without truly experiencing any long-lasting joy, satisfaction or fulfillment. We want to prevent that. It's why we wrote this book.

In my (Joss's) experience over the past 23 years as a seminar leader, businessperson, producer, recording artist, coach and personal manager, I have found, over and over again, that people who seemed to be reaching what seemed to be their dreams were not satisfied. This seemed curious to me, so I have spent many years delving into this area. I have used it as a focus in my work as a coach and personal manager. The answer has become apparent. People do not realize that they already have access to their DreamSource, and they have simply been blocking that access for many years.

WHY WE WROTE THIS BOOK

One reason for this book is to provide you—the reader—with the ability to take away the obstacles between you and your DreamSource so that you can create a powerful foundation, **a place to come from** instead of **a place to get to** in your career.

You will still have specific goals and objectives, but they will be inside of a bigger context. It will not be about needing to accomplish those goals in order to be happy. Being happy will be an integral part of pursuing your goals. This kind of living enables you to be happy and fulfilled when you are catering or working a temp job, as well as when you are on the set of a film or on a Broadway stage.

Another reason we wrote this book is to give the power to the actor. If actors are empowered to take day-to-day actions that are totally and completely up to them, they can start producing results rather than waiting for other people to give them opportunities.

Ultimately this book is about YOU having a fulfilling career RIGHT NOW and being able to pay your bills in the process.

It is easy to say, "Be passionate; be happy; be fulfilled," but one would also logically follow by saying "*How*?" This book will put you on the road to expressing your dreams right now rather than trying to reach them someday, by:

- *creating* value for yourself and others versus *looking* for value out of your interactions and

- clarifying what you are *bringing* to the party (called your career/life) versus what you can *get from* it.

This book will give you the necessary tools to become a walking, talking expression of your DreamSource, which not only leaves you satisfied and fulfilled as an actor, but leaves others around you in a space of being contributed to and inspired.

"You have to learn the rules of the game. And then you have to play better than anyone else."
— **Albert Einstein**

The following diagram explains how acting jobs work, from the initial idea to the wrap party. It is flexible, and although some steps may be bypassed, this is essentially the way everything in New York is done.

- **Producers and writers create projects**.

- Producers hire **Casting Directors** to fill the roles.

- Casting Directors create a **Breakdown** of the roles they need filled.

- Those breakdowns are distributed to **Agents/Managers**.

- **Agents/Managers** submit **Actors** who are appropriate for those roles to the Casting Directors.

- **Casting Directors** sift through the audition submissions and choose some actors to audition.

- **Casting Directors** set up audition appointments through **Agents/Managers**.

- **Agents/Managers** inform actors of those appointments, and the **Actors** confirm.

- **Actors** audition for **Casting Directors** and **Directors**.

- **Directors** choose **Actors**.

- **Producers** okay those choices.

- **Casting Directors** call **Agents / Managers** with an offer of a booking.

- **Agents/Managers** call **Actors** with that offer.

- **Actors** accept or decline the booking.

- **Agents/Managers** negotiate the deal with the **Casting Director** or **Producers**.

- **ACTORS WORK!**

    ***

Chapter 2: The Basic Toolkit

"Keep your dreams alive. Understand to achieve anything requires faith and belief in yourself, vision, hard work, determination and dedication. Remember all things are possible for those who believe."
— Gail Devers

Here is a fleshed-out, made-up example. There are a million variations, but this will give you an idea of how it all works:

Let's say that there is going to be a production of the play *Side Man* at Playmakers Repertory Theatre in Chapel Hill, North Carolina. The Producer (or in this case Artistic Director) of the theatre, and the staff, apply for the rights to the script. Once approved, they decide to look for an actor to play the role of Clifford from the New York market.

Playmakers will hire a New York Casting Director—for example, Calleri Casting. James Calleri, or someone else from his office, will write a breakdown for the role of Clifford. A breakdown describes the attributes of the character that are essential to the role. For example:

Role of Clifford Glimmer: white male, 25-35, frustrated, morose, yet charming New Yorker, who is trying to come to grips with his dysfunctional family.

Then, he'll submit this breakdown to Breakdown Services. Breakdown Services is really the primary service for all things "castable" in the showbiz world. Actors' representatives (agents and managers) receive these breakdowns electronically as they are released, through Breakdown Service's website. Representatives sift through their client lists or "rosters" (the actors they represent) to find appropriate actors for that role. They submit those clients either electronically through Breakdown's website, or they send a hard-copy submission package with headshots and a cover letter.

Over the next 48 hours the Casting Director may receive several hundred submissions for the role of Clifford. Let's say Calleri Casting only has time to audition 30 actors (a completely reasonable number). Now the Casting Director's job gets harder. How does he decide who gets appointments and who has to wait for the next opportunity?

First, they will look at the headshots from the very prestigious talent agencies: Abrams, Gersh and Paradigm, for example. He'll find some pictures he likes, and some impressive resumes, and put them in the "yes" pile. Then he'll go through his own files and pull the headshots of actors he has auditioned before and who have done a good job. He'll put them in the "yes" pile. The "yes" pile is almost full!

Then he'll open up more envelopes and some more virtual files to find more actors who might fit the bill. He won't have time to examine every single submission, and some will go unopened, directly into the garbage. The better the reputation of the Agency or Manager, the more likely the envelope (or the email submission) will be opened.

At this point, Calleri Casting will contact the representatives of the Actors they would like to see audition for the role. He'll give them appointment time slots and inform them of what the Actors need to prepare for the audition.

For example, he'll call Frontier Booking International, a talent agency, and say, "I'd like to see Tim Roberts for the role of Clifford in *Side Man* at

Playmakers Repertory. Rehearsals begin October 1st, and the show closes December 15th. The pay is $900 per week. Please tell him to come to Ripley-Grier Studios for the audition at 11:40 am on August 19th. Have him prepare a short monologue of his choice and the opening monologue from the play."

At that point, the Agent will contact the Actor to relay the information. If the Actor has a Manager, the Agent will contact the Manager, who then contacts the Actor. Once the actor confirms that he will attend, the Agent will call the Casting Director to confirm the appointment. (A hugely time-consuming part of a Casting Director's job is just the scheduling!)

Now it's the day of the audition! The Casting Director, James, arrives at the studio with the Director of the show, and they watch the 30 Actors audition. It's a long day. They decide if they will need to have callbacks or if they've seen enough to decide on their Actor.

In this case, they know from Tim's initial audition that he'd be perfect. James' opinion is very important, but the ultimate decision is in the hands of the Director and/or the Producer of the project. They call Tim's Agent, Frontier Booking, and offer him the role. Great!

Tim's Agent gives him a call with his good news. Tim is thrilled. The Agency is thrilled, because they're getting 10% of Tim's salary. The Agent then calls the Casting Director to accept the role and negotiate the best possible terms for his client.

Tim starts highlighting his script… and the job begins.

***

In most cases, some steps are skipped. For instance, if a small theatre company is self-producing a production of *Twelfth Night* they may not have money for a casting director. They'll just put an ad in a show business periodical, like *Backstage*, and ask actors to send in headshots. (In fact, when you're beginning, show business periodicals and websites are the best way to find work, as you start looking for an agent.)

Twelfth Night's director, and maybe the producer, will look through the pictures and call the appropriate actors for auditions. They may not get the highest quality of actors, but you never know—some of the best performers are still undiscovered.

Remember as well that each audition is a step in building a relationship with all the people involved in the process. You may not be right for Viola in *Twelfth Night*, or Clifford in *Side Man*, but rest assured if you do a good job and behave professionally, you will be remembered when the next project comes up.

Film and television work in very much the same way, except most auditions take place on tape. Auditioning on tape means that casting directors only need you to audition once and your tape can be viewed by all the interested parties: the director, the producers, the studio, the network. Auditioning on tape also gives everyone an idea not only of how you'll perform in the film or show, but what you look like on camera.

Commercials and voiceovers, however, can follow a different process. The agent/manager often has more to say about who gets seen for commercials or heard for voiceovers. Many times a casting director will call an agent/manager and give them a verbal breakdown of what they are looking for and ask the representative to email them a list of names or send their best five. In some cases, the traditional submission process occurs, but often commercials are done from name submissions rather than photo submissions. With voiceovers, many agents have a voiceover booth in their office so they can call in a larger list of their clients and then send only the auditions they feel are appropriate, in a sense acting as a pre-casting director.

Understanding this process is vital to an actor and his own marketing scheme, and typically no one takes the time to explain it to new actors. You can use this chapter and the ones that follow as the **New York Actors' 101 Seminar** you never received when you joined the New York acting community. Welcome.

A career in show business is not like most jobs. In most jobs, you do some work and you get paid for it. Think of your show business career not as a job, but as an entrepreneurial venture. You now own a small business: the business of selling yourself and your talent.

When you own a small business, you have expenses and turn profits. In the initial stages, the expenses will outweigh the profits, but if it is managed well, you'll start to get out of the red and into the black before too long. A good business model will keep the business growing and expanding for years to come. In this section we'll talk about the initial investment, and what you can be doing right now to get your business off the ground.

HEADSHOTS

The first thing you'll need is a headshot. It can be complicated, but don't get overwhelmed. We're here to help. Entire books are written about how to get a great headshot; it's tricky finding the perfect shot. The top photographers in New York can charge (gulp) $1,200 for a sitting.

One cold, hard fact of the industry is that your headshot is your primary marketing tool. You'll have to hand one over at every legitimate audition and every meeting you have with anyone in the industry. You MUST carry them with you to all your professional engagements, even if you think they already have one.

True Story from Guy

I've heard the strangest stories about people being asked for headshots at weird times. A friend of mine was spotted on the 2 train, on a Sunday morning, by a casting director for a Spike Lee movie. She had her headshot. She got the audition.

Okay, since your headshot is your most important marketing tool, you must invest some time and energy in finding the right photographer. When you see another actor with a good headshot, ask him/her who the photographer was. Go to headshot galleries like the one at TVI Studios (www.tvistudios.com) or at The Actors Connection (www.actorsconnection.com). Check out the headshot books at the Reproductions office on 40th St. Look on the Internet. Look in *Backstage Magazine*. Ask casting directors at auditions. Everyone's got a suggestion, and it's actually a great conversation starter.

You may have a really good photographer in another city, but I urge you to find a New York photographer. There is always a style that's in vogue in New York City. Unfortunately, it changes all the time. You need to look like a professional, not like an amateur who is trying to transition from community theatre in Grand Rapids to a career in New York. Even if you don't have a lot of money to spend, spend it in New York.

When you have a list of five or six photographers, you have to interview them. It's yet another tedious chore you'll have to get used to. When you meet potential photographers, you're looking for two qualities: great photos and great chemistry. Each professional photographer should have a portfolio of his work to show you. Part of a photographer's job is meeting with potential clients. Don't be shy; they expect you to ask questions.

***

When looking at a headshot photographer's portfolio, here are some questions you may ask yourself:

- Do I like the pictures?
- Are their pictures consistent?
- Do the actors look good?
- Do the actors look interesting?
- Are the pictures in focus?
- Do the actors look active?
- Is the lighting good?
- Can you see something going on in the actors' eyes?

Here are some questions you may want to ask the photographer:

- How many shots do I get?
- How much time do I get?
- Is it digital or on film? (Film is outdated. Go digital!)
- Do you shoot in color? (Black and white is dead, by the way.)
- Do you shoot inside or outside?
- What kind of lighting do you use? (Natural? Studio?)
- How many changes of clothing do you allow?
- Do we have time to change makeup/hair during the shoot?
- Is there an extra charge for make-up/hair/retouching?
- Will I receive a disc with all images after the shoot or only a select number?

***

If you're getting your first New York headshots, I highly recommend that you go with an inexpensive photographer. You're just learning the style of a New York picture, and you're also learning to look at yourself as a commodity for the first time. There is a really good chance you're going to look at your first headshot in six months and say, "What was I thinking?" You'll be banging your head against a wall if you spent $1,200. If you spent $300 to $500, you can just find another photographer and get more shots.

Here's what your goal is: You want a picture of yourself that looks like you on a really good day—not your best day, just a really great day.

Do yourself a favor: Do *not* take pictures that

have your hair or makeup done in a way that you cannot reproduce. If you get called in for a role, they expect you to look like the photo. This is important. I know it is enticing to hire a hairdresser and makeup artist and look amazing, but if you cannot look equally amazing in "real life," then don't bother. That is not to say that you shouldn't use a makeup artist for your shoot—in fact, if you are a woman, you probably should—but don't go overboard.

You may want several different headshots: one for commercials that is more of a smiling, friendly look, one for soaps that is more seductive, one for film/TV/theatre that is more dramatic, maybe even one for hosting where you look a bit more like a spokesperson. This is, of course, your decision, and will depend on how much money you have to spend. The essentials for starting out are a smiling shot for commercials, and a serious or dramatic shot for theatrical work.

There are many places to get headshots and postcards reproduced. The premier reproduction company is called, fittingly, Reproductions (www.reproductions.com). Their quality is superb, and they are quick, but there are cheaper options: www.ABCpictures.com and www.ISGOphoto.com. You can also get postcards for a very low price at www.VistaPrint.com.

RESUME

There's a classic line from *A Chorus Line* that asks the question, "Who am I anyway? Am I my resume?" Quite honestly, the answer is yes. You *are* your resume and photo unless the casting director has met you and knows your work. That is why it is crucial that the photo captures you and grabs the Casting Director and that your resume is clear and concise. (And yes, you definitely need a resume. A bio is not sufficient, except in certain situations when it comes to reality television or hosting. In these cases, sometimes a bio is preferable because it will illustrate your particular niche expertise, i.e. interior design/law/real estate.)

Just like with headshots, you can find entire books on how to create a showbiz resume. And just like with headshot, there is a specific style to a New York resume. Ask your friends, or people you meet at auditions if you can steal a copy of their resume. Go on actors' websites and download some samples. If you're new to the game and have a fairly empty resume, don't worry! Producers love to take unknowns and throw them into a hit show, and casting directors are always looking for fresh faces. The important thing is not to lie and not to stretch the smallest credits to the point of absurdity.

***

Here are the essential pieces of an actor's resume:

- Name: at the top, with the unions you belong to, if any.

- Contact information: including phone number, email address, and website. If you sign with an agent or manager, you should take your phone number off, and put in their contact info.

- Height and weight: Rounding is okay. Before color headshots, you'd have to include your hair and eye color, but no longer.

- Vocal range, if you sing. Be specific if possible; include your top and bottom pitches. If you don't want to be considered for singing roles, omit this.

- Acting credits: The use of three columns is the most common way to do this. For example, here are credits from a famous New Yorker's resume:

FILM

SISTER ACT	Lead	dir. Emile Ardolino

TELEVISION

WHOOPI	Series Regular	NBC
THE NANNY	Co-star	CBS

THEATRE

A FUNNY THING...	Psuedolus	Lyceum Theatre

You divide the credits up into categories (Film, Television, Theatre, Stand-Up, Improv, Hosting, Internet, etc.). In the first column, put the name of the project. In the second, put the name of the character. If the name of the character is not well known, you put the classification of the role. For example, when Whoopi Goldberg was on an episode of *The Nanny*, she played the role of Edna. In this case, it would make more sense to write "co-star." Other examples of classifications are: Lead, Supporting, Series Regular, Recurring, Guest Star, Day Player, Host, Chorus,

Understudy, Under-five, etc.

The third column is for any additional pertinent information. You can write in the director's name, the production company, the theatre, the network, or whatever makes sense in that space. Don't make it look too all-over-the-place, but a little bit of mismatching in the third column is fine. The general rule is: for theatre, put the name of the theater and the director if he or she is well known; for television, put the name of the network; and for film, put the name of the director.

- **Commercials**: These are not generally listed on actor's resumes. If you have some commercials under your belt, it is traditional to add "List of commercials available upon request." You'll get asked for that list very, very infrequently.

- **Training, Experience and Education**: Especially when you're new to auditioning, this is a vital part of your resume. Write down every degree you have, every class you've taken, every teacher you've had, every internship you've endured, and every name you can drop.

- **Special Skills**: Include dialects you speak, accents you do, instruments you play, and any little thing that you think might get you work. Do you have skills with juggling, rapping, surfing, horseback riding, doing impressions of famous people, cooking? An increasing number of projects require people who are experts in their fields. If you are a lawyer, that's a special skill. Maybe you sew or have childcare experience. Perhaps you're a yoga instructor. Write it down.

Keep the resume clean and up-to-date. Resumes must always be only one page, trimmed down to 8x10, the size of the headshot, and affixed to the back. Staples are the most common way to do this, but we suggest either using double-sided tape or printing the resume directly onto the back of the photo if possible. It's cleaner, greener and it's much less likely that the picture and the resume will be separated.

Casting directors/agents and managers are very busy, they cannot be bothered having to struggle to read or understand a resume. Make it easy for them—not only easy to read, but easy to understand at a glance what you are capable of. There is a sample on the next page.

JANE Q. ACTRESS

Vocal Range: Alto/Mezzo Soprano

TV/FILM
LUCKY FIVE	Principal	dir. Alex Johnson
SYDNEY WHITE	Featured	dir. Joe Nussbaum
STUCK ON YOU	Featured	dir. The Farrelly Brothers
FROM JUSTIN TO KELLY	Featured	dir. Robert Iscove
THE MAGICAL GATHERING	Featured	ABC
CAMPUS MOVIENITE INTRO	Principal	dir. Dan Costa

THEATRE
NEW ROCHELLE	Becky	Footlight Theatre
RUMORS	Cookie	Annie Russell Theatre
MY PAL BETTE	Teacher/Susan	Fringe Festival '07
PLAY IN A DAY '07/'08	Various	Margeson Theatre
EXTREMITIES	Terry	Annie Russell Theatre
ANNIE GET YOUR GUN	Ensemble	Annie Russell Theatre
BABES IN ARMS	Libby	Annie Russell Theatre
THREE VIGNETTES	Laurie	Fred Stone Theatre
A SUMMER DAY IN '42	Cynthia	Florida Studio Theatre
A MUSICAL SEASON OF PEACE	Ensemble	Florida Studio Theatre
ALL HALLOW FRINGE	Tracy Turnblad	Footlight Theatre

COMEDY/HOSTING
LIFE IN STAGES	Host	WPRK 91.5 FM
LADIES WHO LUNCH	Host	WPRK 91.5 FM
CAMPUS MOVIE FEST	Host	Rollins College
AVENUES	Voice Over	Hampton Brown
IMPROVIENTATION	Sketch Player	Fred Stone Theatre
VARIATIONS ON A THEME	Sketch Player	Fred Stone Theatre

SPECIAL SKILLS
Basic Tumbling, Basic Dance, Proficient in Spanish, Guitar, Dialects:
Southern, British, Long Island

EDUCATION/TRAINING
Acting – Thomas Ouellette, Dr. David Charles, Eric Zivot, Kate Alexander,
Beth Duda
Improvisation – Dr. David Charles, Christopher Friday, Joshua Ford
Voice – Eric Zivot, Richard Owens, Michael Horn
Ballet – Madeline Gaston; Tap – Judi Siegfried; Jazz/Modern – Leslie
Brasseux, Dr. Bob Sherry;
Hip Hop – Casper
Stage Combat – Eric Zivot

AUDITION MATERIAL

> "Each man has his own vocation; his talent is his call. There is one direction in which all space is open to him."
> **—Ralph Waldo Emerson**

You're going to learn that your acting talent... is not terribly important.

Well, we're kidding. Mostly. But what is really going to matter when you are starting off is your *auditioning* talent.

When auditioning, you're going to have a few things expected of you: showing up at the right place at the right time, looking neat and appropriate for the role, and being prepared with audition material. In many cases the material will be provided for you when you arrive, or it will have been given to you beforehand. In other cases though, you'll be expected to show off what you've prepared on your own: monologues, songs, and prepared scenes.

Hopefully, if you've ever taken an acting class, you've worked on some monologues, and you have somewhere to start. Find some material, choose monologues and **memorize** them! No ifs, ands, or buts about it! Some of the famous audition books suggest that actors have up to 12 monologues ready at any time. That's craziness. Unless you're auditioning for a full season of work, you'll probably never need more than four, tops: a comic contemporary monologue, a dramatic contemporary monologue and two contrasting classical pieces. For a beginner, though, one good monologue will be fine.

Here is something that shocks most new New York actors: you're rarely going to need monologues when you're looking for work. If you are auditioning for television, films or commercials, the casting people are most likely going to ask you to read a part of the actual script (known as "sides"). If you audition for musicals, you're very rarely going to be asked to do much but sing, dance, and read from the play itself.

Your monologue repertory will come in handy when you're auditioning for agents and managers and attending open calls for non-musical theatre. But you need to know those monologues inside-and-out, and you need to keep them sharp. You never know when you're going to be asked for them.

If you don't have any monologues already in your back pocket, where do you find good ones? Good question! You've probably seen monologue books in the theatre sections of every bookstore. That isn't a terribly good place to look, actually. You're going to want to use your audition time to show what is unique about you. That's challenging to do when hundreds of other people are using the same monologue.

Do some reading. Find great, less famous plays to pull material from. Do a monologue that is from a character of a different sex or ethnic background. Take a passage out of an autobiography. Get creative! I know some actors who even write their own. If that's what you decide to do, you may want to pretend you didn't write it. Writing your own material can come off as cheesy.

If you can't find anything you love, there are always classes around New York that help actors find new monologues, and a private monologue coach can be a great help, too.

INDUSTRY INSIDER:

WHAT IS THE MOST COMMON MISTAKE ACTORS MAKE?

"Air-brushing their headshot photos. The person in the photo should be the person walking into the room. Don't lie or exaggerate on the resume." —*Sue Schachter, Owner, Suzelle Management*

"Not being prepared. Make sure you ask for sides from your agent. Everyone from me to your agent has a lot on their plate and information may slip. Don't blame your agent that you were not told to bring a headshot or you did not get sides. Make sure to cover yourself. Manage your time. If you have an audition make sure you have the time to prep. Skip dinner with your friends and prep instead." —*Sean Desimone, Independent Casting Director*

"They don't take direction. They are too pushy at times." —*Paula Curcuru, President, PMG-Prestige Management Group*

"Thinking you can play anything. It's much more specific and focused."—*Cyrena Esposito, Manager, Red Letter Entertainment*

"Self-criticize themselves while still rolling or even while still in the waiting room. Making a face or similar." —*Susan Gish, Casting Director, Philadelphia Casting*

"They don't listen, whether to direction they are given or to other actors." —*Don Case, President, Don Case Casting*

YOUR BOOK

> "Music is the purest form of art. Therefore true poets, they who are seers, seek to express the universe in terms of music.... The singer has everything within him. The notes come out from his very life."
> —**Rabindranath Tagore**

If you plan to audition for musical theatre, you're going to have to have a "book." A book is usually a three-ring binder filled with audition music (often in plastic sheets). It takes years to develop a strong book. Here are the essentials: a 16 bar cut of an up-tempo song, 16 bars of a ballad and an entire song of your choice.

You never know what else casting people may ask for. Eventually you'll want to include an 8-bar cut of a musical theatre song, a pop song, a country song, a 1950s song, an opera song, a comedy song... and the list goes on. Building your book is going to take a long time, but the best advice is to find music you love to sing, and sing well; that's what will get you jobs.

If you're planning on auditioning for musical theatre, you're going to need to find yourself a good vocal coach. A vocal coach is different from a voice teacher. A voice teacher works on technique, and coach works exclusively on repertoire and helping you sing specific material. A coach helps you find great audition material, and makes sure you sing it well. Coaches run from $35/hr to, gulp, $200/hr. You can find them in *Backstage*, on Craigslist, and through friends and industry contacts.

Even if you think you have a good book, you're going to need a coach from time to time. It's fairly common for you to get an audition that comes with songs that you'll need to prepare. This really sucks, because unless you're a piano player yourself, you're going to have to pay a coach to teach you the material. You may wind up paying $100 to learn songs that won't by any means guarantee you the role. You may even learn songs that you don't get a chance to sing at the audition. It's very frustrating, but it's the way it works.

INDUSTRY INSIDER:

WHAT DO YOU WISH EVERY ACTOR KNEW?

"One, that there is no single, definitive and proven path to success in this business. Everyone is different. Two, no agent, manager, or casting director is going to hold the keys to making you successful. You can't just sit around and hope that some agent/manager/casting director is going to magically procure your dream role. You need to be pro-active and create your own opportunities. You should establish realistic goals for yourself, and then make the effort to accomplish them." —*David Rhee, Theatrical and Commercial Agent, Kolstein Talent*

"How to tell a story, sometimes within 30 seconds, with a beginning, middle and end." —*Susan Gish, Casting Director, Philadelphia Casting*

"Have knowledge about the industry and conduct yourself in a professional business manner. It is a business. One should be prepared with a monologue and or a song to audition when needed. Know your strengths and work towards them. Expect the unexpected, and be willing to pay your dues."—*Eileen Haves, President, Eileen Haves Talent Agency*

"Confidence confidence confidence. There are many good actors, but the ones who book nail the audition. You cannot come across too desperate, which so many do." —*Mark Turner, Broadcast Agent, Abrams Artists Agency*

"The actors get 90% of the money. They have to be willing to do 90% of the work and be proactive. It's a partnership, a team effort, and we want them to succeed. They're the ones who communicate the human condition and take us on wonderful and enlightening journeys." —Ricki Olshan, *Agent, Don Buchwald*

"To have a healthy alternative career that will gratify and support them while they are waiting for their dream to come true. Always have an option in life." —*Sue Schachter, Owner, Suzelle Management*

"The most important thing an actor can know is who they are type-wise and for them to own it." —*Rachel Sheedy, Theatrical Agent, Buchwald*

"How to make the written words their own, and how to listen." —*Don Case, President, Don Case Casting*

"That when you finally get too busy, DON'T COMPLAIN!!" —*Cyrena Esposito, Manager, Red Letter Entertainment*

Chapter 3: Marketing Yourself as an Actor

"You never stop earning when you do what you love."
— **Asha Tyson**

It's time to get down to business. Literally. Starting in this chapter, we will introduce you to tools you can use in your personal marketing plan. You can do each and every thing in the next chapters, or you can choose the tactics that make the most sense to you. The important thing is to come up with a plan, commit to it, and follow through. Let's begin.

MASS MAILINGS

The first tool in your marketing arsenal is the mass mailing. In the Intermediate Kit, we'll discuss target mailings, which are mailings designed with very specific goals. Get used to licking a lot of stamps (or get a wet sponge), because we also suggest sending postcards regularly. Mailings are a big part of your daily work in showbiz.

If you're new, a great idea to introduce yourself to the industry is with a mass mailing. This mailing is going to be tedious and annoying, and expensive, and may make you want to tear out your hair, but you'll only have to do it *one* time. (And if you've been working in the city for a while, you might want to skip this step and go straight on to a targeted mailing.)

True Story from Guy

In my experience, a mass mailing is a great idea for two reasons:

1) You want to be in business with as many people as will have you, and this mailing will introduce you to everyone, and

2) It works. I've done it, and I've had actors I've coached do it to great success.

You're essentially doing the showbiz equivalent of what the advertising industry calls direct mail. You're sending unsolicited mail to a possible customer (in this case, agents, managers and casting directors) with hopes that they'll contact you for your product (you). In advertising, a return of three percent on direct mail is considered good. That means if three percent of the people who receive mail inquire about the product, they would consider that mailing a success.

Go by that three percent rule: if three percent of the people you mail call you – well done! But remember, your marketing will become ongoing and constant. You are starting to establish a relationship with these people (even if it's just them seeing your face for a few seconds). This starts now. That 3% will grow if you keep at it.

The first things you need are the addresses of casting directors, agents and managers. Take a trip to the Drama Book Shop in midtown at 250 W. 40th St. There you can find a periodical called the *Ross Reports* or *The Call Sheet*, which is published every two months with an updated roster of every agent, casting director, production company, etc. that wishes to be listed. It's the go-to guide for names and addresses. It's not the be-all and end-all, though. Some industry professionals don't like their information listed because it leads to too much mail. There is a lesser-known but more comprehensive periodical called *Who's Who in*

Show Business that can also be found at the Drama Book Shop.

Still, there are companies that are hiding from actors. If they are well hidden, that means they don't get much mail. If you get a headshot to one of these hidden companies, your chances of getting a call are much stronger. You have to get crafty. Search the Internet. There are great, and free, actor's resources, that can help you find more names and addresses. Look at the websites for the unions (www.actorsequity.org, www.aftra.org, www.sag.org). Searching for managers is a little bit tougher, because managers are not always listed in the *Ross Reports/The Call Sheet*.

There are also pre-printed lists and labels that are updated every few weeks for sale at various bookshops and online at sites such as www.HendersonEnterprises.com. If you see a Broadway show you think you might be good in, look at the Casting Director's name in the program and put it on your list. Ask your friends.

If you're computer savvy, put all the information into a simple spreadsheet, using a program like Excel. Knowing how to "mail merge" this list with a cover letter will save you a ton of time in the long run. Take the tutorial, and find out how to create "Form Letters." Take the time to do this now; you'll use this skill for the rest of your career.

If computers aren't your strong point, there is always the Actors Fund (mentioned in Chapter 8). One of the things they do is teach basic computer skills classes. I highly recommend that you look into these if you don't know how to use Word and Excel. Not only will it help you with your work as an actor, but it'll also make you more marketable if you ever want to make some money as an office temp.

Now back to the mass mailing. Once you have

your addresses, you have to decide what you're sending. Of course, you've got your headshot and your resume. You must always affix the resume to the back of the picture. You can use staples, glue or double-sided tape. Just keep it tidy and always make sure the resume is trimmed down to 8x10, just like the picture. There is no need for fancy paper. Just make it look clean.

COVER LETTERS

Next is the letter. You should never, ever send a headshot without at least a note. Some people handwrite the note on a post-it, but that's a little tacky. Take this opportunity to write a cover letter that is professional and articulate.

Your cover letter to an **Agent** or a **Manager** should contain the following:

- a greeting
- the phrase "new to the city" or "new to the office" if, in fact, you are new
- two short paragraphs including both professional and personal information about you (Use color and/or bullets to make the important information stand out.)
- a request for a meeting, and
- a closing

Example of a letter to an agent or a manager:

John Shea
Frontier Booking International
1650 Broadway, 11th Floor
New York, NY 10025

Dear John,
Allow me to introduce myself:

- I'm an actor/singer,

- a recent graduate of Northwestern,

- I'm **new to the city**.

- I graduated 2 years ago, and have been working in small regional theatres since then. I recently played Will in a production of Oklahoma at the Marriot Lincolnshire in Illinois.

- I'm finally settled in to my new place in Brooklyn (above a bagel shop that always smells like garlic and cinnamon), and I am ready to start auditioning. That's why I'm writing to you. **I'd love to sit down and talk to you about working together.** Please give me a call when you have time to meet.

Thanks in advance,

John Q. Actor
646-555-1234
JohnQActor@gmail.com

A letter to a **Casting Director** is a little different. Here's why: If an agent or a manager likes your picture and resume, they'll call you in for a meeting. If a casting director likes your picture and resume, they will call you in for an audition. A cover letter to a casting director should contain the following:

- a greeting

- the phrase "new to the city" or "new to the office" if, in fact, you are new

- two short paragraphs including both professional and personal information about you

- a short statement about your type (optional)

- a request that they bring you in for an audition, and

- a closing

Example of a cover letter to a casting director:

Judy Henderson
Judy Henderson Casting
330 W. 89th St.
New York, NY 10024

Dear Judy,

I've lived in New York for several years now. I moved from Texas to become and actress, and before I got much momentum, I got married and had my two daughters. Now they're older and in school, and **I'm recommitting to my dream of performing**.

I'm taking classes and sharpening my skills, and I'd really like to start auditioning more. I'm writing because I'm **new to your office**, and I'd love to be considered for anything you have coming up. If you need a young mom type (some people say I resemble a 30 year-old Marcia Cross), **I'd love to come in and audition for you.**

Thanks in advance,

Jane Q. Thespian
917-555-1234
Jane@JaneQThespian.com

Chances are that most of your efforts will be ignored. Sorry. Agents and casting directors can get hundreds of envelopes a week. If your envelope is even opened at all, you have about five seconds to get their attention, and then they're on to the next one. Use colors, bold type, bullets, include graphics, whatever you can to make them read your message.

A lot of people will tell you to hand-write these kinds of correspondence. That may not be worth your time. When doing a huge mass mailing, that's just more effort than it's worth. Type out the addresses into a spreadsheet, the letter into a word document and "mail merge" them together. Make sure to sign your name though, by hand.

You have the option of printing out labels for the envelopes, but in this case, you *should* hand-write them. It ups your chances of getting your envelope opened. If you are new, then write under the address: "Attn: new to your office".

Another little hint: Don't make your cover letter too big. Think about printing it small, and affixing it to the headshot in the bottom corner with a paper clip. If you do that, the person opening the envelope will have a clear view of your picture. That's your marketing tool. Make sure they can see your eyes as they open the envelope. And, if the envelope has a clasp and a glue closure, just do the clasp. NEVER SEAL THE ENVELOPE. It is annoying for a casting director, agent, or manager to open envelopes sealed with anything other than a clasp.

This is going to be pricey, but it's worth your money, and this is probably the only time in your career you're going to have to do such a massive mailing.

- 200 headshots (not including the initial photo session): $150.00

- 200 resumes, printed and trimmed: $12.00

- Three rolls of double-sided tape to attach the resumes: $6.00

- 200 9x12 envelopes: $17.00

- 200 paperclips: $4.00

- $1.00 postage for 200 envelopes: $200.00

- Total: $389.00

- Getting introduced to the industry: Priceless.

POSTCARDS

We cannot over-stress the importance of postcards.

Show business is all about who you know, right? Well, most new actors don't know anyone. Your job is to meet people, show them that you know what you're doing, and then to KEEP IN TOUCH. Postcards are the way to do that.

When you get headshots printed, also get some postcards. Start with at least 100. They are 4 x 6, and have your headshot on the front. It's a good idea to also have your phone number (or agent or manager contact info) printed on the front. That way, you'll never forget to leave your contact information.

Keep a maintenance list of everyone in the industry that knows you, and might help you get work: directors, writers, agents, managers, casting directors, and producers. Put this list into an Excel file, or handwritten in a binder, or on index cards—whatever works for you.

Every four to six weeks, no matter what is happening, send everyone on your maintenance list an update.

True Story from Guy

I met an agent once, and he wasn't particularly impressed with me. He called me into his office, I sang a song and did a monologue. He never called me again. I still sent him a postcard every four to six weeks for maybe two years. One day I got a call from the man who had been the receptionist when I had had that meeting. I didn't remember him, but apparently I had been nice to him, and he heard me sing through the walls. He'd also been the one who received the mail every day, and he was keeping up-to-date with my career. He called me because he had gotten a promotion and was now a junior agent. He wanted to work with me! Thank goodness I have been sending cards.

On a more mundane level, postcards are a reminder that you're out there, and eager to work. It also shows that you're organized and disciplined, and that matters to agents and casting directors.

The postcard should include:

- A greeting
- An update. Include any and all bookings, or callbacks if you had no bookings. And if you have nothing new to report, fudge it. You can stretch the word "recently."
- A request. For instance, ask an agent for a meeting, or ask a casting director to keep you

in mind.

- Some sense of personality. Make it personal.

- Contact information

Schedule time for this every four to six weeks. Don't forget. You list may be small to start with, but it will grow. A consistent postcard mailing system will be a huge help and will yield huge results. *I believe it!*

Here's an example of a postcard:

To Judy Lesley, Sinclair Management

Dear Judy,

I hope you had a great holiday. I sure did, but it's great to be back in the swing of things.

I'm just writing with an update: It's been getting slow in the legit world for me, so I **signed up for an improv class** at the Upright Citizens Brigade.

On the commercial side, **I booked two on-camera commercials** recently (a foreign language school, and a car website).

Looking forward to the coming year! **I'd still love to meet with you.** Please give me a call when you have the opportunity to chat!

All the best,

Jane Shakespeare
646-555-1234
Jane.Shakespeare@yahoo.com

THANK YOU CARDS

"Saying thank you is more than good manners. It is good spirituality."

—Alfred Painter

In the business world, every time you have an interview, it is polite and smart to send a thank you note, especially if you really want the job. Every audition you go on is an interview. A thank you is often appropriate.

You may see actors leaving an audition room, and writing the thank you note right there, in the waiting room. They drop it in the mailbox on the way home. There is something to that, but writing thank you notes for EVERY audition may not be a great use of your time and money.

A rule of thumb is: send a thank you note if it's the first time you've met someone, or if you've had a really significant experience in the room. If you audition for a casting director who really works with you and guides you so you nail it for the producers, then that's worth a thank you note. If you are auditioning for a casting director you see all the time, and this was not a special audition, then skip it.

It's important that a thank you note is just that: a note of thanks. Be careful not to ask anything of the recipient—that's just basic good manners. For example:

But what all do you say?
should you say?
can you say?

To Craig Burns, Bernard Telsey Casting

Dear Craig,

I just wanted to say thanks again for calling me in for *HAIR*.

The opportunity to audition for the show was a thrill, and I really appreciate the notes you gave me. They made the callback feel **so much more focused and relaxed**.

Thanks, Craig.

Linda Stanislavsky ちち ha!
646-555-9876
LindaStan@aol.com

      You can send a thank you note on a picture postcard, or you can buy regular thank you notes at a stationary store. Just make sure that your picture is included too. Either fold a picture postcard into the note, or include a photo business card. *I need cards pen!*

      By this point, if you are new to acting you probably never realized how much "office work" is involved in being an actor. But we are not done yet! The key is to make your mailing different and attention-getting. Every casting person or agent receives hundreds of photos and resumes each week. Why should they open yours, and why should your photo not go into the "circular file" (otherwise known as the trash can)?

      You have to make your letter, photo, envelope, package, etc "stand out" in some way.

True Story from Joss

One time an actor sent me a dollar bill and written on a sticker on the bill was the sentence, "Let's make money together." I put her headshot aside and eventually called her in because it stood out as different.

Of course, if you have an amazingly good photo, that can be simply enough to get a call, but most people are not so unbelievably gorgeous and stunning that the person opening their photo cannot resist the urge to call them. Most people are more ordinary or usual looking. Their talent may be unusual and extraordinary, but talent is rarely communicated through a photo. This is why it is crucial to come up with a way to have your mailings compel a casting director, manager, or agent to call you in.

You want the person to think, "I should meet this person." Even if they do not call you in right away, or ever, if you do a memorable mailing, your next contact with that person can reference it and their memory will be triggered. Repetition is sometimes the key to getting in the door.

True Story from Joss

I had someone mail me postcards periodically for over a year while meanwhile asking her friends, who were my clients, to put in a good word for her, until I finally met with her and then subsequently signed her.

You need to make it EASY for someone to say yes. If this is an art that you master, there will be no limit to your success in anything you are doing.

Make it easy for someone to say yes and you will get a lot of yeses.

INDUSTRY INSIDER:

WHAT IS THE MOST EFFECTIVE WAY FOR AN ACTOR TO KEEP IN TOUCH WITH YOU WITHOUT BEING ANNOYING?

"If an agent requests that an actor do so, send a postcard with specifics and helpful information about having gotten a role (not about auditions, call backs, or what they had for lunch)." *—Cici Qiu, Agent, Don Buchwald*

"By emailing once every month or so." *—Paula Curcuru, President, PMG-Prestige Management Group*

"Picture postcards and sometimes through email."

—Eileen Haves, President, Eileen Haves Talent Agency

"A postcard or email is fine with an update. I also have a Facebook group where actors can write on my wall or post in the group. You don't need to contact me every time you book, so save up your mailings and outreach for when you have a few announcements. Also keep in mind it's my job to know who you are, so I will think of you when a project comes up that you are right for. I always go back to my files of past projects." *—Sean Desimone, Independent Casting Director*

"Email with updates of actual updates, but don't just say, 'I'm checking in.'"*—Mark Turner, Broadcast Agent, Abrams Artists Agency*

"Postcards and/or a note. But I don't think it's really necessary. If someone auditions and I'm impressed, I'll stay in touch with them....trust me. Do not phone or email. Emails and phone calls from actors is the worst!"
—*Don Case, President, Don Case Casting*

"Still, the old-fashioned postcard in the mail. NOT email." —*Susan Gish, Casting Director, Philadelphia Casting*

"I insist that they call in at least twice a week, usually between 4-6pm. They should know they have a relationship that needs communication. Always call and book out when you are not available."—*Sue Schachter, Owner, Suzelle Management*

*Note: Do not email an agent or manager unless they give you the okay to do so. Unsolicited emails tend to piss people off.

SUBMITTING YOURSELF FOR PROJECTS

"The greatest danger for most of us is not that our aim is too high and we miss it, but that it is too low and we reach it."

— **Michelangelo**

Even if you have an agent or manager, it is critical that you do you own research on what is being cast and, in many cases, prepare your own submissions. Reviewing the casting section in *Backstage* (in newspaper format which comes out every Thursday, or online at www.backstage.com) is an easy way for actors to learn about castings and to submit themselves

for projects, and most actors do this on a regular basis.
There are many other web-based casting services, such
as Actors Access, produced by Breakdown Services,
and *The Buzz*, that allow actors to submit themselves
for projects. Checking these websites and submitting
yourself for projects is a critical component of the
actor's job, and some of the most successful actors
have, at one point in their careers, made this a daily
habit.

These are just some of the websites you can check:

- www.ActorsAccess.com (without a doubt the best)
- www.Backstage.com
- www.NYCasting.com
- www.Mandy.com
- www.Craigslist.com (many people have booked huge gigs from here)
- www.ExtrasAccess.com
- www.SAG.org (look for casting)
- www.ActorsEquity.org (all Equity gigs are listed)

A good way to remember to check these is to give
yourself alerts. Using Google Calendar, or AOL
Calendar, you can send yourself emails, once a day, or
once a week, reminding you to check these websites.
You can also use www.MemoToMe.com for this
purpose

Chapter 4: Intermediate Toolkit

> "Ah, mastery... What a profoundly satisfying feeling when one finally gets on top of a new set of skills... and then sees the light under the new door those skills can open, even as another door is closing."
> —**Gail Sheehy**

So far, we've gone through the basics. You've got your headshot and resume. You've got your audition material. You're submitting yourself for work, and you've got a mailing system in place. The Intermediate Toolkit chapter will help you figure out some more advanced marketing strategies that can move you forward at the quickest pace possible.

YOUR WEBSITE

Nowadays, it is simply bad business for you not to have a website. It is simple and inexpensive to set up, and you can even do it yourself if you have no budget. Actors spend anywhere from $0 to $10,000, but the simple fact is YOU SHOULD HAVE A WEBSITE.

A website not only makes your agent/manager's job easier, it gives you someplace to show additional photos, reviews, voiceover samples, tape from film/TV projects, and other information that is not appropriate for a resume. Your web address should be on your resume, and you should keep it as updated as possible. You can list dates of shows, TV appearances, commercials you have booked, etc. It is a way to create a view of you as a professional working actor. Even if you do not have performances scheduled you can create a website that makes you look more in demand than you really are, if need be.

True Story from Joss

I cannot tell you how many times websites have come in handy when speaking to casting directors or producers who were under pressure to find someone for a role. The fact that I could send them to a client's website so they could see what the actor looks like or watch their reel, was the reason they booked the job or got the audition.

GET A WEBSITE. No excuses. For the cheapest options, consider using the templates at angelfire.com, GoDaddy.com, or i Web for Mac. You can also use sites like MyActingSite.com, which is simple and easy to use.

DEMO REEL: PUTTING ONE TOGETHER

TAPE TAPE TAPE. It is an invaluable tool in helping you get an agent. Even if you have an agent, tape can help them market you to casting directors and producers in a way that your headshot/resume cannot.

Sometimes it is hard to gather and accumulate tape when you are starting out. Many people do student films, commercials, and TV shows and then find it difficult to get the tape, either because the projects don't get completed or the directors/producers simply won't send a copy.

The minute you book a student or independent film, commercial, TV show, etc., you need to be thinking about how you are going to get the tape. The tape is the only documentation of your work on that project. If you do not get it, no one will make sure they send it to you.

If you are representing yourself, once you book

the job see if you can get it put into your contract that a copy of the tape needs to be provided. When you go on set, at an appropriate time, find out who the producer is and get a contact number for them or for the director. The producer will be the leverage point for you to ultimately get a copy of the tape on any commercial, independent film or student film.

A standard demo reel is around 3-5 minutes long and can contain any number of clips. Be smart about putting your best foot forward with the clips you choose. Of course high quality footage is impressive, but don't worry about film quality too much. Most demos are watched on computer screens; they don't have to be in high definition. They just have to be clear enough to see and hear you.

If you do a TV show or soap, then the best bet without cost to you is to make sure someone tapes it when it airs. Most television shows are available for a cost from the production company after it airs, but it is cheaper to simply videotape it yourself on a high quality tape/DVD, or ask a friend to do it for you.

For many actors who are just starting or actors who specialize in theatre, there may not be tape available. In this case you have two choices: either wait until you do something and get the tape to create a reel, or make it yourself. The latter is not the preferable method, but it can certainly be an alternative.

You could put yourself on tape with your home video camera (making sure it looks good) doing a monologue or scene or sides from an audition piece that shows your range. You could actually get together with some other actors that need tape and produce a short film that features you. You can go to many services that cost approximately $50.00 and they will put you on tape doing a scene or monologue.

You can also buy a video camera for $100 to

$150. A video camera is an invaluable tool for an actor. It enables you to not only put yourself on tape but also to immediately upload that tape to the Internet to be emailed to your agent, manager or casting director. This will enable you to have something to show people. Although excerpts from actual work are always better, at least self-produced tape can show you acting.

True Story from Joss

I always tell my clients to get a small video camera. The FLIP Cam is the easiest to use in my opinion. Many times the opportunity to put themselves on tape and email the audition to casting arises. My client Chaske Spencer booked the role of Sam Uley in the *Twilight* saga using the Flip camera in my daughter's bedroom. That camera is the best money he ever spent.

As far as distributing your reel, if you are shopping for an agent and have a reel, sending out DVD copies can be very effective. This gives people a chance to see your work, again making it easy for them. The worst kind of letter is one that says, "If you are interested in seeing a reel, contact me." This is absurd. Of course seeing a reel is better than not seeing a reel.

If you have a reel, SEND THE REEL. And/or have the reel on your website and include a link to your site in your cover letter so that they may view your work. Requiring that the agent contact you to get a reel is too much work. They may not want to invest the time or effort. If you have already sent it, the chances of them watching it at some point are far higher than the chances of them calling you to ask you to send it.

VOICEOVER DEMO REEL

Voiceovers (VO) have a really high income-to-effort ratio. It's just about the least amount of work you can do, for a great amount of money. You can roll out of bed, and record a voiceover in your pajamas in ten minutes that could appear in a national commercial or radio campaign and make you $100,000. And you didn't even take a shower.

So how do you get into Voiceovers? The first thing you'll need is a voiceover demo. Good voiceover demos are usually between 60 and 90 seconds, and contain four to ten clips of commercial copy. Ideally, you would use clips of things you had actually booked in the past, but if you don't have any, it's fine to use clips of things you find yourself. A demo can also have different tracks (an animation voice track, a narration track, a promo track), but most people will start with just a commercial track.

Stick with your strengths on a demo. Don't use six different accents. Casting directors usually look for native speakers when they need accents, so they are authentic. Instead, use copy from commercials you could see yourself booking with your natural voice.

Now, where do you get a demo and how much? A lot of the studios that record commercials provide services for actors who want to create demos. (Google Shut Up & Talk and Edge Studios for examples.) In most cases, you can take a one-night class or a group class, and find out a little more about the business. That's a great place to start. You can also go to www.voicebank.net and hear some really great professional demos.

Much like with headshots, price and quality vary drastically from office to office. A demo can cost between $200 and $2,000. We urge you to start with a cheaper demo, and once you start auditioning, go back for a higher-end version.

True Story from Guy

I did my first demo for $400, and after six months of auditioning realized I had done it all wrong! Some of the choices I'd made were very amateurish, and I had my type all wrong. I thought I sounded 25-35 (good for bank commercials, car ads, etc.), but it turns out I sounded 18-25 (good for fast food commercials, toys and games, and cable companies). After a couple dozen auditions I had a much better idea of what casting directors were looking for, and I decided to use that knowledge to make a stronger demo. The second one cost me $1,200, but it was the single best investment of my career. It paid for itself within a year, and it opened my career up to tons of possibility and tons of money.

Once you have a demo, do a target mailing to voiceover agents (see below). Almost every agency with a commercial department submits actors for voiceovers as well. In some cases there is a dedicated VO agent, but if not, just send them to the commercial department.

You'll often hear that voiceovers are hard to break into, or that 100 VO artists are making all the money. That used to be true, but it's changing quickly. First of all, there are tons of non-union commercials being cast and none of the big-time VO artists can even audition for them. Second of all, the aesthetics have changed, and casting directors are always looking for fresh voices.

Don't forget to send postcards to your VO contacts. Put them on your maintenance list, and keep them updated every four to six weeks.

TARGETED MAILINGS

> "Efficiency is doing things right; effectiveness is doing the right things."
> —**Peter Drucker**

We've already mentioned mailing schemes in this book. In the Beginners Kit, we went though how to do a mass mailing, which is useful for new actors to introduce themselves to the New York market. We also advocate sending postcards every four to six weeks.

There is one more type of mailing that is a key to accomplishing your goals: a Targeted Mailing. You do a targeting mailing with a smaller goal in mind: I'd like a commercial agent, I'd like a voiceover agent, I'd like to be seen for primetime pilots, etc. In this case, you mail to a much smaller, targeted list, but you do it much more aggressively.

Let's say your short-term goal is to find a commercial agent. First, do your research, both by using periodicals and by asking anyone who will listen, "Which agencies would be a good match for me?" Compile that small list, maybe 15 agencies, and make a plan of attack. Though most offices share files, pick one person in the office and mail to him or her. The following plan, for example, has been quite successful.

- <u>Week One</u>: Send a headshot and cover letter. (See the cover letter examples in the Beginners Kit.) Be specific about what you want, for example: "I am looking for commercial representation. Please call me so we can talk about working together." If you have a reel, put the DVD in the envelope. Register for a commercial class, so you can put that in the cover letter. Be aggressive, and make it easy for them to say yes to you.

- <u>Week Three</u>: Send a postcard with any new information. Reiterate the reasons you'd be a good match and request a meeting again.

- <u>Week Five</u>: Do it again. Another postcard with updates and a request.

- Now you can back off, but only a little. Add these names to your postcard maintenance list, and send them a postcard every four to six weeks for the rest of your career.

- <u>Weeks Six to Ten</u> (Optional): This is the perfect opportunity to use meet-and-greet classes to your advantage. Search through the schools that offer one-on-one classes with these agents. Try: <u>www.actorsconnection.com</u>, <u>www.thenetworknyc.com</u>, <u>www.breakthroughstudios.com</u>, <u>www.one-on-one.com</u>. And register to meet them.

- If you can schedule a seminar, send yet another postcard. Let them know that you're going to be meeting them in person. Say, "I registered for your seminar, and I look forward to meeting you at Actors Connection on September 15th." The agent will be looking for you; you've already established a relationship, and the agent will see how eager you are.

If this kind of aggressive mailing doesn't get them to notice you, nothing will! The same schedule of mailing can be applied to any subset of the industry: managers, primetime casting, etc. It's a really cost effective way to make your short-term goals a reality.

AUDITION LOG: EYE ON THE BALL

An audition log is just that: a log book of all your auditions. In it, you list the vital details of the audition: the project, the casting director, the material you performed, whether you got a callback, etc.

We highly recommend getting clear about your DreamSource prior to going into any audition or meeting (Chapter 6 will help with that). This will give you a place to focus other than on getting the job. If you play basketball with your eye on the scoreboard, you will not be very effective. Keep your eye on the ball (in this case your DreamSource) and no matter how it all turns out, you will be fulfilled **right now**. This is something you have 100% power over. Whether or not you book the gig will be up to a myriad of factors, but your satisfaction is up to you.

True Story from Guy

I have kept an audition log since my first audition in New York, over 1,250 auditions ago. I can't tell you how useful it has been. For me it's also a great motivator. I'm really proud of going on that many auditions, and it makes me feel like I'm really working hard to make my career happen.

First of all, an audition log is a great way to keep track of your progress. You have to keep your business growing and advancing. How are you going to track that progress without records?

When you go on a theatre audition, always write down what you performed in the audition and what you wore. If you get called back, you want to make sure you don't perform the same material, and why give the casting director the chance to mix you up with another actor? Wear the same clothes. Theatre Casting Directors always say it helps them out when you wear the outfit that you first auditioned in to your callback. It helps them remember who you are. If you get the callback, spray some Febreze on your audition outfit, and wear it again. It's less important to repeat the outfit when you're doing an on-camera audition. (It's tough to get you confused with someone else when you're on tape.)

You should also write down the name of the casting director and director, in case thank you notes are appropriate, or if you would like to add them to your Maintenance Mailing list. If you meet an assistant, write their name down, too. Today's assistant is tomorrow's boss.

You can tailor your audition log to what suits you best. For the best use of your money, just buy a small, hardbound book and make your own log. A soft notebook will fall apart. Here are some suggestions of what to track:

Audition Log

Date: Audition #:

Name of Project:

My DreamSource (what I intend to leave the casting director with):

Casting Director:

      (add to mailing list?)

      Address:

Director:

      (add to mailing list?)

      Address:

Submitted by whom? (agent/manager/self)

Wardrobe:

Pieces Performed:

Who I met:

How did it go? What did I leave them with? Was my DreamSource present for them/me?

Notes:

Callback? Y/N   Book it? Y/N

For example:

Date: Apr 15, 2010   **Audition #:**1234

Name of Project: *The Bald Soprano*, an Off-Broadway play.

My DreamSource (what I intend to leave the casting director with): SELF EXPRESSION AND JOY

Casting Director: Bettina Bilger Casting

> **(add to mailing list?)** NO
>
> **Address:** already on my mailing list

Director: Kate Middleton

> **(add to mailing list?)** YES
>
> **Address:** c/o Ground UP Productions, 72 Barrow Street #2N, New York, NY 10014

Submitted by whom? (agent/manager/self)

Barbara at Barbara Andreadis Talent

Wardrobe: Grey suit, blue shirt, and no tie

Pieces Performed: Monologue from *The Maids*

Who I met: Bettina's assistant, Rebecca Hoberman.

How did it go? What did I leave them with? Was my DreamSource present for them/me?

Solid! Director loved the sides. Everyone in the room was present to joy and not only my self-expression but their own! The director even laughed out loud four times.

Notes: Need to find a shorter/funnier monologue. Quick!

Callback? YES   **Book it?** YES

20 THINGS YOU CAN DO WHEN YOU FEEL STUCK

1) Volunteer in a casting office. When you meet a new casting director, ask them if they ever need readers or assistants. Readers are the audition assistants that read audition scenes with the actors who come in. It's a great way to get to know the casting people, to show that you know how to act, and to demystify the process, so that you're much more relaxed next time you come in for an audition.

FUN FACT FOR AUDITION ASSISTANTS: When Harrison Ford was starting out as an actor, he took up carpentry to support his wife and children while he was waiting for his break. In a stroke of fate, director George Lucas hired Ford to build cabinets in his home and ended up casting him as a small but pivotal role in *American Graffiti* (1973). Two years later, in 1975, Lucas used Ford to read lines for actors being cast for parts in his upcoming space opera, *Star Wars*. At the reading, Steven Spielberg noticed that Ford was well suited for the part of Han Solo and convinced Lucas to give Ford the role.

---

2) Volunteer as an intern to do some office work with your agent or manager. It can be really eye opening for an actor to see exactly what goes on in the office all day. The actors get to know their reps better, and vice versa. This relationship is crucial. Why not spend some time on it?

3) Take a class. Improv, Stand-up, Storytelling, Voiceover, Shakespeare. There are 1000 great classes in the city. Classes will sharpen your talent, they will

help you network, and they will give you something to put on a postcard.

4) Go to the gym.

5) Write a short film script. The book *Screenplay* by Syd Field is the classic how-to manual on screenwriting.

6) Organize an actors' support group with a few of your friends to meet once a week and work on new material. A support group can help you work your audition material, sharpen your mailings and correspondence, and hold you accountable for your marketing plan. When you set a goal and tell everyone about it, you're much more likely to put the work in.

7) Submit yourself for five things you would not normally submit yourself for.

8) Learn a new monologue.

9) Organize your expenses to date so you are better prepared for tax season.

10) Write a thank you to your agent or manager for no specific reason, just for their partnership in causing your success.

11) Read a play you have never read before.

12) Pick your favorite actor. Rent three movies he/she is in, and have a movie marathon.

13) Register to do background/extra work. Being an extra is boring, yes, but it pays and gives you the opportunity to work on a set. If you're not comfortable with how a film/TV/commercial set works, then do some extra work and learn the lingo. You can register with the big background casting directors either by mail or open calls.

14) Go to an open call you wouldn't normally attend. Open calls are great ways to gain experience and the perfect venue to debut a new monologue you've been preparing.

15) If you sing, prepare a song and tape it for your website or to send in CD form when you do mailings.

16) Hold a staged reading in your apartment. Cast your friends in all the roles.

17) Research improv and/or theatre groups and submit yourself to five.

18) Videotape yourself doing a scene or monologue and watch the tape. Look to see what works and what is missing.

19) Learn a new accent so you can add it to your repertoire. The standard way to do this is to buy practice tapes at any drama bookshop, but thanks to the magic of youtube, you can also find free lessons online.

20) Start an AFI film club with your friends. Go to AFI's website and pick one of their many "Top 100" lists, then start working your way down the list, watching the movies. Pay special attention to studying the performances.

Chapter 5: What Work is Available?

"You come to New York to find the ambiance that will evoke your best. You do not necessarily know precisely what that might be, but you come to New York to discover it."
—**Dr. James Hillman**

People always say that if you're bored in New York, then you're just not paying attention. Robert Moses once said, "Every true New Yorker believes with all his heart that when a New Yorker is tired of New York, he is tired of life." This town is the beating heart of so much, and as a New York actor, you have many advantages in your court, merely because of location.

From Broadway to TV and Film, from comedy to cabaret, New York is the best place in the world for entertainment. That's why you brought your career here. As a performer, the opportunities are vast. Here is a breakdown of what work is actually available to you.

THEATRE

There is no better theatre than in New York City. With about 40 Broadway theatres, and hundreds of off-Broadway, and off-off-Broadway theatres, New York has more opportunities to perform than any other city in the world. The flip side is: there are tons of actors as well, all vying for those roles. The competition can be fierce.

Let's start at the bottom. Once you explore the theatre scene in New York as an audience member, you'll discover the huge diversity of shows and performances. All of the performances spaces that are not classified as Broadway, or off-Broadway, are lumped into the category "off-off-Broadway." Off-off-Broadway can include anything from huge theatres in Queens to tiny outdoor spaces in Fort Tryon Park to converted office-spaces in the East Village.

In 2008, at the Innovative Theatre Awards, which celebrates excellence in off-off Broadway theatre, legendary playwright Edward Albee was one of the presenters. He regaled the audience with stories of his early career and the freedom he found working in off-off Broadway. He said there are two types of theatre in New York: "commercial theatre, and theatre that matters." For Albee, off-off Broadway is where the real creativity is.

Independent companies produce the large majority of New York's off-off-Broadway theatre: groups of like-minded artists who use their time, effort, and sometimes their own money to make a show happen. These shows very often use only non-union actors, because they can't afford to pay actors the minimum required by the Union. If it's an Equity Approved Showcase, then Union actors are allowed to perform for a tiny stipend, but many companies won't go through the trouble of dealing with Equity.

Getting cast in your first off-off-Broadway show can be thrilling for a new New York actor. Warning! You never know what you're going to get. Some off-off-Broadway projects are legit. For instance, the musical *Urinetown* premiered off-off Broadway in 1999, and by 2001 it had moved to a Broadway house with some of the original cast. Other off-off-Broadway shows can be disorganized and agonizingly difficult. Be smart about how you choose to spend your time, especially when working for free.

Publicizing a role in an off-off-Broadway show is an excellent way to market yourself. If the show is good, do a mailing and invite everyone in the industry who might be able to find you work. If the show is bad, you can at least send out the information on a postcard to your industry list. Agents, managers and casting directors want to know that: a) you're practicing your craft, and b) someone thought you were good enough to cast in a show.

In order for a production to be classified as off-Broadway, it has to be housed in one of the theatres classified by the League of Off-Broadway Theatres and Producers as an off-Broadway house, and it has to adhere to the guidelines of the trade unions that govern the actors and technicians.

There's a lot of variety in the scope of these shows. At the Abingdon Playhouse on 36th Street, you could have a small theatre company doing an original play, trying to attract producers to bring it Broadway. At the Minetta Lane Theatre, you could have a musical with millions of dollars in funding that requires a more intimate setting than a large Broadway house would allow.

Accordingly, getting a role off-Broadway happens in a variety of ways. There may be open calls. There may be ads on the Internet asking you to send in a headshot. You may only be able to get an audition through an agent or a manager.

The most frequently asked question in New York is probably, "How do I get in a Broadway show?" The answer is not simple. There are only about 40 Broadway houses, and with the exception of the one at Lincoln Center, they are all located within a few blocks of Times Square. Getting cast in a Broadway show is most often the culmination of years of practice and a powerful marketing plan. In all cases, Broadway shows have open call auditions called Equity Principal Auditions (EPAs), but most of the casting happens

68

through private casting directors, by appointment only.
If you want to book Broadway gigs, you need to find
yourself a powerful representative to get you in the
door.

FILM AND TELEVISION

"Film is one of the three universal languages, the other
two: mathematics and music."

—Frank Capra

When it comes to film and television, the major
market is Los Angeles, but there is still work to be had
in film and television in New York. The amount of
work varies, year to year, for a handful of reasons. The
city of New York offers tax credits to production
companies that work out of New York, but the amount
of the credit goes up and down, and the city doesn't
always promise that the tax laws will remain in effect
from year to year. Because of this, production
companies don't always love working in New York.
There are a few series, and quite a few films, that shoot
in New York, but the number of productions varies
considerably.

Nowadays, on sets in and around New York,
the tax credit is a regular topic of conversation. How
much? Will it stick around? Why doesn't the city
realize the amount of money and the number of jobs
the film industry brings to New York every year?

As far as television goes, New York is the
home for several primetime series such as (as of 2009)
the three *Law and Orders*, *30 Rock*, *Gossip Girl*,
Damages and *Ugly Betty*. Two daytime dramas are
taped in New York: *As The World Turns* and *One Life*

to Live. There are also quite a few other series, including *Saturday Night Live*, *Late Night with David Letterman*, *Good Morning America*, *The Today Show*, and *The Daily Show*. You can consult the *Ross Reports/Call Sheet* for a full list of programs filming at any given time.

Casting for these New York shows mostly takes place in New York. Often each show will have a dedicated office, and one casting director who is in charge of the entire casting process. Building relationships with these people is the best way to get seen for auditions and book work on television.

The biggest and best gig in television is, of course, being a series regular on a primetime show. The good news is that even if a show isn't filmed in New York, if the producer is a big operation (Warner Brothers, CBS, HBO) they will almost always cast in both Los Angeles and New York. Very often, the New York branch of the casting office will search through dozens, if not hundreds, of actors and put the best on tape to send to LA. You'll often hear the New York casting offices complain that the LA offices have much better luck, because it's much easier for actors to impress producers in person in LA, than in a QuickTime file sent from New York. However, each and every year, you will see New York actors in the high profile pilots.

Traditionally, television pilots (the first episode of a series, produced as a test to see if the series is any good) were shot between January and April of each year. This was known as pilot season. After the writers' strike of 2007-2008, and with the prominence of cable series and year-round original programming, pilot season has become a lot more spread out. Pilots are shot all year round now.

The film industry in New York works largely

the same way as the television industry. However, you can't always count on a big budget New York film being cast in New York. It's very common for the large roles (if not all the roles) to be cast in LA. It's not uncommon however, for the smaller roles to be cast locally.

Luckily for actors, New York is home to a huge amount of smaller, independent films. Dozens of films are cast each month that have smaller budgets, but are great ways for actors to cut their teeth. For a lot of these films, you'll need an agent/manager to submit you, but that's not always true. Sometimes there are ads in showbiz periodicals and online for you to submit yourself. It's still true that LA is the place to be if you want to be a movie star, by if New York is more your lifestyle, there is good work to be had.

COMMERCIALS AND VOICEOVERS

"It's important to have a voice; it's more important to use it."

—Anonymous

Because most of the nation's biggest advertising agencies are located in Manhattan, New York is the best place for an actor to find work in commercials and voiceovers. There's a booming commercial industry in LA, but it's about half the size of the one in New York.

Plus, the money in the commercial industry for actors is huge! If you're a principal in a union commercial, you not only get a handsome day rate for when you shoot the spot, you will also get paid a residual every single time it airs, in any market, on any channel, at any time of day. The exact math of how much you make per airing is incredibly complicated, and well watched-over by the unions. Suffice it to say, actors have made a great deal of money from commercials.

True Story from Guy

At one of my first commercial auditions, I'd signed in and sat down and two minutes later, Broadway star Norbert Leo Butz walked in and did the same. At the time he was in a Broadway show, *Wicked*. In fact, he had originated the role of Fiyero. I was thinking, "Why is Norbert Leo Butz auditioning for commercials?" The answer was this: he could have made more money from one day of work filming a national commercial, than several weeks of work on Broadway. That information really changed the way I thought about the business.

In order to be a principal in a commercial, you must speak, touch the product, or be integral to the action of the commercial. You are also a principal if your voice is heard and your body is not seen. That's a commercial voiceover.

Commercial voiceovers, in addition to radio voiceovers, are another huge business for actors. You may not even notice, but there are voiceovers in almost every television commercial. The umbrella of voiceover also includes audio books, telephony (see Glossary), and animation. There is a lot of money to be made there. In order to get a voiceover agent, you will probably have to make a voiceover demo reel, which was previously discussed in the Intermediate Kit.

Commercials and voiceovers may not be

glamorous, but they are vital to your success as an actor in New York. Do you know the actor Billy Crudup? He was in the movies *Watchmen* and *Almost Famous*, as well as almost a dozen Broadway plays. Did you know he is also the voice of MasterCard, the one who does the "Priceless" voiceovers? He's been quoted as saying that if it hadn't been for the money from commercials, he would have been forced to quit acting before he ever got the chance to take off. While he was sharpening his skills, and building relationships with people in the industry, he was paying his rent with commercial money. The point is – don't turn your nose up at commercials. They can be your lifeblood.

HOSTING

Hosting opportunities for actors have really grown over the last few years. Consider, for example, how many more reality shows there are now than there were ten years ago. They all need hosts. New York is home to several minor cable channels, like The Discovery Channel and Nickelodeon. They use hosts all the time.

Hosting requires a good stage presence and an ability to quickly develop a good rapport with people. If this describes you, you may be perfect for a hosting gig. Nowadays the trend in hosting is experts. If you are truly an expert in something (finance, law, exercise, nutrition, relationships, etc.), hosting can be a good market for you.

Some of the larger agencies have agents dedicated only to actors interested in hosting, but in most cases, the legit/theatrical agent will handle these kinds of auditions. Much like in voiceovers, the first step is usually a demo reel.

OTHER WAYS TO WORK

"If you're not sure what to do with the ball, just pop it in the net and we'll discuss your options afterwards."
—**Bill Shankly**

If you've come to New York with an intense passion to perform, there are countless ways you can do that. New York is home to a vibrant comedy scene. If you enjoy performing stand-up, there are over 20 clubs. A lot of comedy clubs have open mic nights or "bringer" shows, where you get stage time in return for bringing a few people with you. Many clubs also have stand-up classes, which are a great way to start. If you are an improviser, there are a ton of schools and performance venues. Sketch comedy is also alive and well in New York. Check out classes and shows at places like the Upright Citizens Brigade or The People's Improv Theatre for classes and performing opportunities.

New York is the home to at least five of the country's best film schools. And film students are always looking for actors for their projects. In fact, there is no better way to get experience on film than by doing student films. Further down the line, you're going to need to create an acting demo reel for yourself. Start immediately by collecting clips of yourself acting in student films. These clips are the first building block.

The best student films are made at NYU. Columbia's films are the next best. Films made at The School for Visual Arts, and The New York Film Academy may not be as strong. A gentle warning: when dealing with student directors, you may sometimes get frustrated with their lack of experience. Also, student filmmakers are notorious for not finishing projects. Keep after them to get a copy of the film, or at least of your scenes for your reel and website. When you work for free, they at least owe you that.

Let's say you're a thespian, but you can't seem to get hired for the roles you'd like to play. Produce the play yourself! There are easily over 200 self-produced shows in New York every year. All you need is a group of like-minded artists, a script, and some production money. That sounds simple, but of course it's not. Fundraising can be very difficult, as well as finding high quality actors, designers and technicians who are willing to work for free. That doesn't stop people from trying.

Creating your own production in order to showcase yourself is another cornerstone of good marketing for actors. If you want to show the industry that you can give a great performance, then give yourself the opportunity. Then invite everyone in the industry who might possibly help you get ahead. This is a great way to find an agent, and a great way to impress casting directors.

In short, although acting in New York triggers the knee-jerk response of thinking "Broadway," the opportunities span far beyond that.

Chapter 6: The DreamSource

> "True happiness is ... to enjoy the present, without anxious dependence upon the future."
>
> **— Seneca**

What are you ultimately committed to accessing or achieving? Do not say an Oscar or a Tony or $5 million a year. This is not a question about an increased salary or an ideal role, but rather a particular sense of being.

What brings you satisfaction? After you reach all the goals, get all the jobs, and the awards, and the money, what will be available at the end of it all? What emotion, what qualities of life or ways of being? What is inspiring you right now to push toward your acting goals?

The answer to that question is what we are calling your DreamSource.

THE NEXT CARROT SYNDROME

> "Each morning when I open my eyes I say to myself: I—not events—have the power to make me happy or unhappy today. I can choose which it shall be. Yesterday is dead; tomorrow hasn't arrived yet. I have just one day, today, and I'm going to be happy in it."
>
> **— Groucho Marx**

Mules are notoriously stubborn. Farmers were forever frustrated by their mules, which would stop in the middle of plowing a field or pulling a cart, and refuse to budge. One day, an enterprising farmer rigged up a stick with a carrot on a string attached that would dangle in front of his mule, a few inches from its nose. The mule single-mindedly started moving toward the carrot, but because of the contraption, it could never get close enough to take a bite, and from that day forth, mules have continued plodding steadily forward, trying to "catch up" with the carrot.

Not to say that humans are as dumb as mules, but we are certainly as stubborn, and just as prone to chasing the unattainable as it dangles enticingly out of our reach.

There is always a "next carrot," something that pops up as the be-all and end-all thing to obtain after you have obtained the previous be-all and end-all result. This is the nature of being human—or an actor. Nothing is ever very satisfying for very long.

The problem with this is that it's a perpetual cycle that leaves you with little satisfaction, or only with satisfaction for short blips of time. It is a normal tendency to look at certain people who appear to have what you want and say, "If only I were X," or "Look at X; he really has it all."

We promise you that if you talked to X, you would find that they are chasing their own carrots, just at a level distinct from yours. Consider this trajectory of thought:

- If only I had a great headshot.

- If only I had an agent.

- If only I had a bigger, more powerful agent.

- If only I had my Equity card, my SAG card, my AFTRA card.

- If only I had a national commercial running.

- If only I had a role on a soap.

- If only I had a contract role on a soap.

- If only I had a primetime series.

- If only I had a series regular role on a primetime series.

- If only I had roles in movies.

- If only I had bigger roles in movies.

- ...and so on and so on.

It never ends. There is always another "if only." No matter what level of success you reach, the next level looks better than where you are now.

Yes, the grass is greener, but in reality, you are always where you are now; always on the grass you are on at this very moment; always at the level you are at now; always the weight you are now; and you always have the representation you have or don't have now.

You always have the life you have RIGHT NOW.

You are never actually at the next level you are craving, except for that very brief moment when you "cross over" to the next level. And yes, for that brief moment, there is the joy, freedom and power of being ahead of yourself. But then reality settles in, and you are once again faced with craving the next level. Still you are ALWAYS exactly where you are NOW. That is the dilemma we face with the current model that most people live inside of.

What if you could have access to being satisfied, powerful and fulfilled, right now? Not *when* you get the soap, or the film, or the series, or the Oscar, or lose 10 pounds, or get the big agent, but right NOW. What is it that you are really after? If it is not ultimately the soap, the series, or the Oscar, what is it? It is the feeling of attaining it. The feeling of power, success, elation, and satisfaction.

This is your DreamSource. Operating from your DreamSource, versus following that next carrot, will leave you satisfied and fulfilled right now, not someday, not when you book that X or win that Y. A fulfilling career now? Yes, no matter what the circumstances.

DREAMSOURCE: A DEFINITION

"Success is not the key to happiness. Happiness is the key to success. If you love what you are doing, you will be successful."

—Herman Cain

We have dreams as children, and those dreams are wild and unfettered and lovely.

If a little boy wants to be a firefighter, he does not think, "I have a dream to be a firefighter, but the test is so hard and the rescues are dangerous, and the program is competitive and the hours will be difficult for my family." If a little girl wants to be a princess, she does not think, "I have a dream to be a princess, but it will be difficult to find a prince to marry, and I will eventually need to take over the kingdom and learn the politics of ruling a country, and I will have to spend the majority of my time granting pardons and making summons and staving off war."

No, the young boy thinks of rescuing babies and dogs bravely from inside a raging inferno and emerging unscathed. The young girl thinks of riding bareback on unicorns in long, gossamer gowns. When we are young and pure, we think anything is achievable, and it is a joyful, satisfying time.

As a child, achieving the dream is not

important. We were joyful and satisfied simply by the dreaming process itself. We did not worry about how we would do it or if we would do it, because our state of being was calmed by the fact that we had that dream. That dream itself was a source of fulfillment and joy.

We are happy being dreamers. As we get older, we become "realistic," "reasonable," and "mature." In other words, we "grow up," and that sense of happiness, fulfillment and power is often overshadowed by concern, doubt and fear. Actors are notoriously large dreamers by nature. It is a profession whose pursuit can be wrought with rejection, disappointment, aggravation and endless worry. To survive the rejections, to pursue and push and practice until you are the best, to audition endlessly, to maintain your health, to believe with your entire heart that you will—you *must*—succeed: that requires a strong base of optimism and faith. To be an actor is to be, by definition, a dreamer.

Imagine if you could be the way you were when you were four years old, unencumbered by the concerns, fears and reservations that descend upon you as you grow older; not limited by the circumstances or content of your adult life, but able to be powerful, satisfied, free and fulfilled in the face of any circumstance. That is what is available to you as an actor if you identify and rediscover your DreamSource and create opportunities to express it in your daily life.

This is not to say that you do not come up with a plan to accomplish your intended goals. On the contrary, creating your DreamSource gives you a place to come from when developing that strategy. When you are coming from a place of power, the plan you create takes on a whole new life. You will be taking actions from a totally different place. *This will enable you to produce results that are satisfying, but it does not require you to produce the results in order to be satisfied.*

Being an actor is inherently frustrating in terms of who makes the decisions. It seems as though it is up to everyone but *you* as an actor. But you can bring your DreamSource to every interaction, audition, mailing, meeting, booking and performance. You will no longer try to get satisfaction from the casting director or the agent or the manager or the booking. This enables you to be in the position of power.

Our commitment in writing this book is to put the power back in the actors' hands, so that not only are they in action in achieving their dreams, but they are in action from a new place that has them be powerful, joyful and fulfilled in the process.

You will still need to take the appropriate actions, of course. It will be with even more passion and power that you are able to embark on your goals so that your satisfaction becomes a RIGHT NOW phenomenon, rather than the next carrot that you are chasing.

TRUE STORY FROM JOSS:

How I Discovered My DreamSource

> "To succeed, you need to find something to hold on to, something to motivate you, something to inspire you."
> **—Tony Dorsett**

When I was four, all I wanted to do was be a singer. I would make up songs and put on shows in my garage with my friends. It was very clear to me that not only did I *want* to be a singer, but I was *going* to be a singer and have a hit record. It did not even enter my mind that it would not happen.

My father was an advertiser, but he loved to paint in his spare time. When I was five years old, I was sitting with him in our 1968 Chevy convertible and I asked him why he stopped painting as much as he used to. He said, "Well, you can't do your art as your career." In that moment, the world changed for me. It became a place where "you could not do your art as your career." My art was my singing. In the infinite wisdom of a five-year-old, I decided that was the way it was—after all, my dad said so. As early as eight years old, I remember when a grown up asked me what I wanted to be when I grew up, my answer was no longer a singer. It was a lawyer. That seemed more realistic, reasonable and mature.

Although I continued to sing throughout grade school and high school, I decided to go to college for business. I had put a lid on my dream, hoping it would go away. It never did. I got a job as a producer, but I decided that I had to sing, even if it was in my spare time, so I started to put together cabaret shows every few months. It was fun; I was able to sing but still have my "real life." My friends and family would come to the shows and it was good enough. And then, in 1990, my brother Bruce died of AIDS.

He was my champion. He directed my first cabaret show, he bought me my first Ella Fitzgerald album. He always said, "Sing." I always said, "Someday."

When Bruce died, I was on my way to visit him at the hospital. I had not visited him the night before, and I remember saying to myself that I would go tomorrow. When I got the call that he had passed away, I realized suddenly that there is no guaranteed tomorrow. So why do we all live like there is? We live as if there is a someday, but there is no someday.

Today is it. Now is all we have. It was the time to start singing. It took me 17 years to override my father's absolute truth that "you can't do art as your career" and ask myself, "What if I *could* do art as my career?"

I began introducing myself to people as a singer, which at first seemed like a lie. Struggling was not my thing, and I had no interest in making it my thing. So as I began to exercise the muscle of telling people I was a singer, it felt a bit like "fake it till you make it." At first I would say, "I am a singer...but I am also a producer," or if they would ask, "Where do you sing?" I would answer, "Well, I am planning a show…." It all felt very uncomfortable at first, but after a few weeks during which I scheduled a show and made a demo and took other actions consistent with being a singer, it got easier and easier to say I was one.

Two months in, I received a phone call from a woman who said she was a manager. She was putting together a band called Boy Krazy, a girl version of New Kids on the Block. She had heard I was a singer. Was I interested? I had to laugh a little, because it actually worked! She heard I was a singer from someone I told I was a singer in the previous eight weeks. I, of course, said I was interested and met with her and the record label. It was between me and another girl who was 10 years younger than me. I spent four days calling everyone I knew asking them to concentrate all their wishes and thoughts and prayers on "intending" for me to get it. My friends in California, my sixth grade teacher, my grandparents. I had over 70 people "intending."

Meanwhile, this was a very fun four days. In fact, it was probably the most alive, free, excited, powerful and joyful I had felt in a while. It was not so much about getting the deal, but the very dream process.

After a series of meetings, playing them my demo and endless phone calls, they told me that I was their first choice to complete the group. OH MY GOD, MY DREAM COME TRUE!!!!!!! It was like a miracle. I was on fire.

Of course after the initial excitement, the reality settled in and the "next carrot syndrome" set in. Okay, I thought, I have a deal, but now we have to make a great record. We made a record, released it in England and it flopped. Okay, I thought, maybe a different record. We released another one in England and it flopped. Obviously we needed new management, I thought. We got it. No good.

The record company was going to drop us. Then the record started to get popular in the U.S. The company decided not to drop us, and we climbed the charts, replacing Whitney Houston's "I Will Always Love You" as the Number One song in the country in March 1993. It seemed like a fantasy.

But the next carrot syndrome kept kicking in. Now we need a follow-up song, I thought. We released one. It flopped.

The point here is that there is always a next carrot. The happiest, most fulfilled and satisfied I ever felt was before I even got the deal—the days of the dream process, the days of "intending."

"Happiness is inward and not outward; and so it does not depend on what we have, but on what we are."
—Henry Van Dyke

When I met my husband in 1994, I discovered that what was important to me now was no longer being a pop singer, but being a wife and mom. I left

Boy Krazy, got married and had my daughter Sophie—again, fulfilling my personal dream. I continued to produce commercials part-time, wrote songs and jingles from time to time, and raised my daughter. When she was two, I began to search for a new mission.

I had the life I had always dreamed of. I had a great family, I had accomplished the #1 record, produced hundreds of TV shows and commercials, and I had led seminars and courses for thousands of people to help them accomplish their dreams. Whenever I was leading courses, I found myself in that dream process again. I was totally satisfied and fulfilled just to be in the process of having people create their lives with me, having people fulfill their dreams. It felt like home.

It became clear that this was my DreamSource: helping people fulfill their dreams, helping people's dreams come true, helping people be self-expressed, powerful and fulfilled. That is what inspired me, that is what fulfilled me, and it was not about the reaching of a goal; it was about the dream process itself.

When I realized this, I started my personal management/production company and called it *Reve*, the French word for dream. It made sense that I should create a career out of making people's dreams come true. I have since changed the name to Josselyne Herman and Associates, but the heart is the same. I have been able to create a career that is a daily expression of my DreamSource, giving me the opportunity to access that joy, fulfillment and satisfaction on a right-now basis. I am doing my art as my career. I am living my dream.

HOW TO FIND YOUR DreamSource

"Whatever you do, or dream you can, begin it.
Boldness has genius and power and magic in it."
—Johann Wolfgang von Goethe

First it is important to identify the model you are currently in by answering two questions:

- **What** are you trying to get?
- **Where** are you trying to get?

For some people this is a very complicated process; for some it is crystal clear. There are many ways to identify your DreamSource. In fact, you may already know what it is from simply reading this far. We will go over two methods of uncovering your DreamSource in this book.

Wherever you are in the process is fine, just allow yourself to notice your answers to some of the following questions, and feel free to write your answers in the spaces in this book.

METHOD ONE

"You are worried about seeing him spend his early years in doing nothing. What! Is it nothing to be happy? Nothing to skip, play and run around all day long? Never in his life will he be so busy again."
—Jean-Jacques Rousseau

Go back to when you were young, four or five years old. See if you can picture yourself then. What did you want to be when you grew up?

What were your dreams?

What did you LOVE to do for endless hours as a child?

See if you can get back to that time and actually experience what it was like as that four or five year old. What qualities are present? Is it freedom? Passion? Joy? See if you can articulate the qualities that are actually present, as you are simply being the four or five-year-old dreaming about being a movie star, fireman, pop star, ballerina, etc.

Notice that the qualities that are present are not connected to actualizing the dream, but simply that the **dream process** itself evokes those qualities. See if you can capture the essence of what is inspiring in a few phrases or sentences. Fill them in here:

Now pick the two or three words that encapsulate your previous answer. When you are able to capture the qualities that your dream process evokes in one, two or three words, that is your DreamSource. Write that down here:

Remember this is etched in sand, not stone. You are not stuck with anything you come up with, and you can always change, add to and modify what you come up with right now.

***

Guy's Response to DreamSource Method One

Go back to when you were young, four or five years old. See if you can picture yourself then. What did you want to be when you grew up?

A baseball player. As it turns out, by the time I was about 8, I learned I had NO talent for it.

What were your dreams?

I remember dreams of being in the spotlight, literally. I don't know how I got there, or why; I just remember the spotlight. Warm and loved.

See if you can get back to that time and actually experience what it was like as that four or five year old. What qualities are present? Is it freedom? Passion? Joy? See if you can articulate the qualities that are actually present, as you are simply being the four or five-year-old dreaming about being a movie star, fireman, pop star, ballerina, etc.

Pride, independence, hope, safety, tranquility.

Notice that the qualities that are present are not connected to actualizing the dream, but simply the **dream process** itself evokes those qualities. See if you can capture the essence of what is inspiring in a few phrases or sentences. Fill them in here:

I think that I could easily imagine that pride I'd feel if I just had the opportunity to be a baseball player.

It never occurred to me that I wouldn't be amazing.

Now pick the two or three words that encapsulate your previous answer. When you are able to capture the qualities that your dream process evokes in one, two or three words, that is your DreamSource. Write that down here:

Being calmly confident and proud.

Elisa (Actress)'s Response
to DreamSource Method One

Go back to when you were young, four or five years old. See if you can picture yourself then. What did you want to be when you grew up?

I remember singing all the time. In class, I would read out loud in very animated voices, as if I was storytelling. My grandmother called me "Squirrel" because I was always jumping all over the place, from one pillow to another. I was imaginative, always lost in my own world. In third grade, I remember writing my own songs. I used to tape myself singing over pop songs from Belinda Carlisle and Debbie Gibson, dreaming of being a recording artist.

What were your dreams?

Just to be happy and to sing. I wanted to take lessons like all the other kids. I did some, but not enough. I went to a private school with a long day and a long bus ride, and my parents were too busy to cart me around. When I was in the fifth grade, my father heard on the radio that the local

community center was doing *Fiddler on the Roof*. I was 11, but I lied and said I was 14 and they cast me as an adult part.

See if you can get back to that time and actually experience what it was like as that four or five year old. What qualities are present? Is it freedom? Passion? Joy? See if you can articulate the qualities that are actually present, as you are simply being the four or five-year-old dreaming about being a movie star, fireman, pop star, ballerina, etc.

Absolute freedom. I was in LOVE with music and playtime. I was aware of tension in my house between my parents, and I internalized that to escape into plays. Such freedom! I remember playing Dorothy in *The Wizard of Oz* at summer camp when I was ten, and the day after the play was over and camp turned back into regular camp, I was completely sad and depressed.

Notice that the qualities that are present are not connected to actualizing the dream, but simply the **dream process** itself evokes those qualities. See if you can capture the essence of what is inspiring in a few phrases or sentences. Fill them in here:

I would say I was insulated in my dreams. I didn't care what anyone else thought, and I was confident that I had all the time in the world. I felt so unconditionally loved by everyone in my life.

Now pick the two or three words that encapsulate your previous answer. When you are able to capture the qualities that your dream process evokes in one, two or three words, that is your DreamSource. Write that down here:

Insulated, confident, hopeful, loved.

Bernadette (Actress, Host, Author)'s Response to DreamSource Method One

As a child, I enjoyed making up dances, writing poems, stories, songs and acting out little scenarios on "why you mustn't smoke cigarettes" or "why you must dance a lot everyday" (because it makes you laugh!) and then dancing for everyone, always being the emcee, always being the "front person," organizing and enhancing the info for everyone's ears and enjoyment... so my three words are INSPIRE, ENTERTAIN, IGNITE. Which is exactly how I proceed today with my Health and Nutrition mission, as well as author, intuitive counseling and acting roles. All that was already there for me as a little girl!

Yvette (Actress)'s Response
to DreamSource Method One

Go back to when you were young, four or five years old. See if you can picture yourself then. What did you want to be when you grew up?

A singer/actor/dancer/entertainer and a veterinarian.

What were your dreams?

I loved music and wanted to have my own radio show and be a singer. I also loved to dance. I knew from a young age that I would grow up and make a

difference in people's lives.

See if you can get back to that time and actually experience what it was like as that four or five year old. What qualities are present? Is it freedom? Passion? Joy? See if you can articulate the qualities that are actually present as you are simply being the four or five-year-old dreaming about being a movie star, fireman, pop star, ballerina, etc.

Freedom, laughter (happiness and joy), playfulness, freedom from worry, encouraged, invincibility.

Notice that the qualities that are present are not connected to actualizing the dream, but simply the **dream process** itself evokes those qualities. See if you can capture the essence of what is inspiring in a few phrases or sentences. Fill them in here:

I felt unstoppable, free-spirited. I was bursting with creativity, excitement, passion, inspiration, fulfillment and happiness. I felt that no matter what I wanted in life, I could go out there and get it!

Now pick the two or three words that encapsulate your previous answer. When you are able to capture the qualities that your dream process evokes in one, two or three words, that is your DreamSource. Write that down here:

Creativity and inspiration.

METHOD TWO

"It is not how much we have, but how much we enjoy, that makes happiness."

—Charles Spurgeon

When you think of your career, what is your immediate goal?

If you accomplished that goal, what would be available in your life that is not currently available?

Now let's say you had everything you just listed. What would now be available for you that was not available before?

Now let's say you had all of that, as well, everything you just wrote in your latest answer. What would now be available for you *now* that was not available before?

Again, let's say you had all of that previous answer. What quality of life or way of being would *now* be available for you that was not available before?

You could ask yourself this question many times before coming to your DreamSource, but at the end of the questioning, you will find it. If you could paint the canvas any way you wanted, this is what you would paint. If you could trade in everything, this is what would be worth it to you.

Guy's Response to DreamSource Method Two

When you think of your career, what is your immediate goal?

To make a living in the industry.

If you accomplished that goal, what would be available in your life that is not currently available?

The money and freedom to travel and buy all the things I want.

Now let's say you had all of that, everything you just wrote, what would now be available for you that was not available before?

The time and peace-of-mind I lack from being so busy working and/or panicking.

Now let's say you had all of that, everything you just wrote, what would now be available for you that was not available before?

Complete pride, and complete tranquility.

Benjamin (Actor)'s Response
to DreamSource Method Two

When you think of your career, what is your immediate goal?

To advance my acting studies (Shakespeare, the Classics, etc.) and to have a speaking line in a major TV or film. The "dream" which I, ironically, came very close to in the past year was getting back into pop recording, which was something I tried hard to do in high school.

If you accomplished that goal, what would be available in your life that is not currently available?

Validation from my family, a larger impression among my non-actor friends, and I'd probably feel a little more secure around my boyfriend's movie star friends!

Now let's say you had all of that, everything you just wrote, what would now be available for you that was not available before?

I would feel more assured that I was on the right track and that I would not be "regretful" of time I wasted not doing exactly what I wanted to do. I was also really happy when I was working part-time at a survival job last year. Being full-time in a job that is not artistic is a real killer. I would love to be part-time again. I think I have a lot to offer companies, and I am really smart, so I would always want to work some sort of job. Why not? You always need extra money.

Now let's say you had all of that, everything you just

wrote, what would now be available for you that was not available before?

Relaxed and happy.

Your DreamSource may very well be your best access to creating a fulfilling, powerful career as an actor, as well as a satisfying, joyful life as a human being.

If the whole point of everything, when all is said and done, is to be self-expressed and passionate, then why not have it *NOW* versus once you have a television series? Not only should you ask yourself, "Why not now?" but also, "If not now, when?"

It is a myth to think that the series will give it to you, that the casting director will give it to you, or that being famous will give it to you. There are countless examples of how that myth breaks down in reality. Just look back to your youth. It was all about, "When I get to high school," or "When I get a boyfriend/girlfriend," or, "When I don't have to listen to my parents," or some version of that. Then it was, "When I go to college," or, "When I get out of school and get into the real world," and then "When I get 'the' job." Then you get the job, and it is about "When I get the better job," or maybe, "When I get the relationship," or, "When I lose 10 lbs," or, "When I meet the right agent/manager," or, "When I book that gig." Which pretty much brings us up to date.

Nothing has changed. Now is the time to break out of the next carrot syndrome and start creating a career that is satisfying, powerful and fulfilling *now*. It is time to find your DreamSource and start **bringing it to your career** rather than hoping to get something from your career that is impossible to obtain.

Change always begins with an honest assessment of self. The next few exercises will help you openly and honestly assess where you are at in your career, what characteristics and beliefs you have that are holding you back, and what characteristics and beliefs you have that will help you move forward and succeed as an actor in New York.

EXERCISE ONE

"A master in the art of living draws no sharp distinction between his work and his play; his labor and his leisure; his mind and his body; his education and his recreation. He hardly knows which is which. He simply pursues his vision of excellence through whatever he is doing and leaves others to determine whether he is working or playing. To himself, he always appears to be doing both."

—Francoise Rene Auguste Chateaubriand

List the results you have produced in the past six months in your career. Include everything you can think of. Every class you took, every audition you attended, every reading you performed, every role you booked or lost, every contact you have made, every play you have read, every monologue and song you have memorized.

Now list all the results you have produced in the past year.

In the past three years.

In the past five years.

What results did you intend to produce by this time that have not yet been realized? List them.

Write down the reasons you tell yourself for having not produced those results yet, including whose fault it is.

What is the answer to the following: "If I only had **X**, those results would have been produced?"

Take some time to read over what you just wrote. Everything you have written down—all the results you have produced (of which there are probably far more than you realized), as well as the things you did not produce—all of it is behind you now. You can be proud of what you have accomplished, of course, but it is not true that you "should have accomplished" what you have not accomplished as of yet. Believing that gives you no power.

You have accomplished more than some people and less than others. Okay, so now what?

There is absolutely nothing you can do to impact any of it at this point. What you can do is let it be however it is, and start from right now. Start fresh. This is what you have to work with. These are the accomplishments. This is the education and training. These are the contacts. Now what?

It is time to create the career of your dreams, NOW. What will it take to be an expression of your DreamSource on a day-to-day basis? What will it take to be satisfied and fulfilled as an actor, now? It will take discipline. It will take work. It will take exercising the DreamSource at every possible moment: from the moment you wake up, to when you get your coffee, to when you do a mailing, to when you audition, to when you work with your acting partner, to when you call your agent, to when you walk down the street.

This is something you can bring to your entire life that will start to become who you are, rather than merely something you are trying to become.

EXERCISE TWO

There are many actions that you can take to strengthen your DreamSource muscle while it is still new. After a period of time, you will not need all of these reminders, because it will begin to be who you are innately. But for now, take as many opportunities as possible to remind yourself of your DreamSource. Fake it till you make it on this one. Consider some or all of the following:

1) Consciously focus on who you are being in

every interaction, and ask yourself continuously, "How can I bring my DreamSource to this interaction?"

2) Write your DreamSource on your day planner.

3) Tell your closest friends and family about your DreamSource so they can support you in bringing it to interactions with them.

4) Use it as a screensaver for your computer.

5) Put it on a post-it on your fridge, front door, etc.

6) Write it in dry-erase marker on your bathroom and hall mirrors.

7) Have it be your phone message screen when you turn it on.

8) Find or create a physical object that symbolizes your DreamSource and look for a physical place to keep it as a reminder.

9) Set up email reminders with your Internet provider to send you an email everyday with a message to remind you of your DreamSource.

10) Make it your ring tone, so that every time your phone rings, you hear it.

11) Create an association with a particular color that reminds you of your DreamSource, and make sure you have something in that color that you access frequently (wallet, key ring, scarf, gloves, bag, etc.).

12) Find a song that reminds you of our DreamSource. Keep it on your phone or iPod and play it every day at least once.

EXERCISE THREE

"Don't look back on happiness or dream of it in the future. You are only sure of today; do not let yourself be cheated out of it."

—Henry Ward Beecher

List the areas of your life to which you are already bringing your DreamSource.

In which areas are you stuck?

What are the reasons you tell yourself you are stuck in those areas?

In those areas, come up with three ways to remind yourself of your DreamSource when the going gets tough.

EXERCISE FOUR

"Take up one idea. Make that one idea your life. Think of it, dream of it, live on that idea. Let the brain, muscles, nerves, every part of your body, be full of that idea, and just leave every other idea alone. This is the way to success, that is the way great spiritual giants are produced."

—Swami Vivekananda

Many times, people are not clear on how people view them and therefore unable to be fully expressed or powerful. There may be areas in which people perceive you exactly as you would want them to. There may be areas in which you would be very surprised to find out how people perceive you, or ways in which you would not want to be perceived. The point of this exercise is to discover an accurate and honest impression of yourself, to determine whether or not you need to work to shift the impression. Knowing where you are will allow you to get to where you are going more effectively.

Write down what you believe people say or think about you, as both a person and an actor. Be straightforward with yourself, and try to capture your strengths and weaknesses as honestly as possible.

- What do you think your agent says/thinks about you?

- What do you think your manager says/thinks about you?

- What do you think casting directors say/think about you (both the ones who have cast you and the ones who have not)?

- What do you think your actor friends say/think about you?

- What do you think your non-actor friends say/think about you with regard to your career?

- What do you imagine your parents say/think about you with regard to your career?

Time for a reality check. Call them up. Explain that you need honesty. Tell them you need the truth—the good, the bad and the ugly—in order to address and minimize your weaknesses and play up your strengths. Write down what they say next to your answers above. Compare, and ask yourself the following questions:

- In what areas were you close?

- In what areas were you far off?

- Were there things that you were surprised to hear?

- Did anyone have a much more positive opinion that you imagined they would?

- Did anyone have a much more negative opinion than you imagined they would?

- Based on the answers you received, what is one thing that you need to work on? What are two steps or actions you can take immediately to begin working on on that one thing?

- Acknowledge your strengths: what are two things that you do very well?

These exercises are designed to support you at any time, so feel free to do them periodically. You may be surprised that what you see each time is not the same thing you saw the time before. Give yourself space to discover new things about who you are and what inspires you.

Chapter 7: The Team

"Our success has really been based on partnerships from the very beginning."

—Bill Gates

Michael Jordan holds the NBA record for highest career regular-season scoring average (30.12 points per game). Can you imagine if he scored 28 points in a game and in the post-game interview he said, "Thanks, but I really wish my teammates would score more baskets. It's a shame; maybe if I had better teammates we would win more games." Or if they lost a game and he said, "I've been thinking about leaving the team. The point guard doesn't pass me the ball as much as I would like, and the coach just doesn't get who I am." That would be absurd, wouldn't it?

But how many times have you heard an actor say, "My agent isn't sending me out as much as I want," or "I have only had X auditions, so maybe they are not very well connected? If I had a bigger agent, that would make the difference."

In this chapter, we are going to talk about all of the contributors to your success as an actor (photographer, agents, managers, coaches/teachers, family, directors, crew, casting directors, casting assistants, messengers, interns, etc). As you pursue a career as a New York actor, using the tools and methods introduced in previous chapters, keep in mind that there is no one person who makes or breaks your success.

If a job is booked, it is the result of the power of the team. So let's talk about the key players.

> ### INDUSTRY INSIDER:
> ### WHAT MAKES A GOOD CLIENT?
>
> "A good client has the whole package, the talent, energy and passions for the work. He or she is always prepared for auditions, has read the material, is familiar with the director's work, learned the sides, is fully present and focused." —*Ricki Olsha, Agent, Don Buchwald*
>
> "Dedication to your craft, drive, motivation and integrity are essential. You must present yourself honestly at all times, be easy to work with and take direction well. Also, confidence (but not arrogance)." —*Eileen Haves, President, Eileen Haves Talent Agency*
>
> "Someone who is hard-working and entrepreneurial and sees themselves as partners in their career." —*Rachel Sheedy, Theatrical Agent, Buchwald*
>
> "A good client is one that books."—*Mark Turner, Broadcast Agent, Abrams Artists Agency*

If someone were investing in your business, how would you speak to him or her? How would you work with them? How would you think about them? It can alter your relationship with your representation, or your quest for representation, if you shift how you view the relationship.

Your agent/manager is putting forth a tremendous amount of time and money on the chance that you will succeed. It costs a lot of money to represent someone. There is the cost of Breakdown Services, subscriptions, phones, office, Internet, envelopes, postage, messengers, supplies, entertaining casting directors, and all the other costs associated with representing someone. This is not inexpensive, as you know by how much you spend on your own headshots, occasional mailings, etc. Your representation WANTS you to succeed. They WANT you to get auditions. They WANT you to book.

Next time the internal desire arises to complain about your representation or lack of auditions, remember that they do not get paid until you work as an actor. They are investors in the business of you, and you need to treat them as such in order to get the most out of the partnership. With this in mind:

Instead of asking yourself:	Ask yourself:
How can I get my agent to send me out more?	How can I make myself more casting director friendly?
How come they can't get me in the door of the casting office?	How can I help my agent or manager to get me in the door of the casting office?
Why won't they see me for this role? I'm perfect for it!	What can I do to separate myself from the hundreds of other actors being submitted for the very same roles?
Why doesn't my agent/manager have more influence? Maybe I should be with a bigger agency.	How can I make sure that when the casting director sees my photo, they will give me an audition time?

Remember: If there was an athletic event between a unified team and a single player, the team would win every time, no matter how talented the single player is.

TIP: IT IS CRUCIAL TO ACKNOWLEDGE THE SOURCE OF YOUR RESULTS: the team of people working to create those results. When you stop acknowledging the source of your results and start thinking you are doing it all on your own, you stop getting those results. You cannot source yourself.

AGENTS VERSUS MANAGERS

As an actor, when you hear the term "representation," sometimes this refers to an agent, sometimes a manager, sometimes both. What is the difference? Do you need both?

Agents

Think of an agent as an employment agent. Their job is to get you appointments for job opportunities. That is their primary function, and most of them do it quite well. This business is primarily about relationships. Agents have spent years creating relationships with casting directors. Agents have negotiated deals for years and know what to ask for, even when you don't. They also know when not to ask for things, which can be incredibly useful. A good agent can be invaluable in creating the career of your dreams.

Agents are bonded and licensed by the state, and they have the ability to freelance with as many actors as they like. An agent often works with a much larger client list than a manager. They also tend to specialize: dealing with just theatrical work (theater, television, film), commercials, hosting, voiceovers or print. They generally get 10 percent of all contracts (except for print work, which is typically commissioned at 20 percent). Additionally, if an actor is signed to a contract with an agent rather than freelancing, the actor is not allowed to work with any other agents in that particular area of specialization.

One question you should ask yourself when seeking an agent is whether you would prefer to be with a large agency or a boutique one. There are benefits to both.

Clearly, finding the right agent depends on a variety of factors, such as agency size, and your skill set, type, chemistry, experience, etc., but the most important thing is finding an agent who is genuinely excited about you as an actor. If they are not, it does not matter if you are with one of the top agencies or a boutique firm. If your agent is personally invested in you and your career, then you will get someone working for you who will go the extra mile, or make the extra phone call and the extra pitch. That enthusiasm can sometimes be worth more than a fancy logo; however, casting directors sometimes only work with a short list of agencies based on their relationships. The point is THERE IS NO PERFECT AGENT. There is just who is the perfect agent for you.

Managers

A manager's job is to coach, counsel and advise an actor, and to manage the team of people responsible for the actor's success. It's often said that actors need managers most at the beginning of their career and at the peak of their career. At the beginning, an actor needs to build relationships with agents and casting directors, and no one can make that happen more effectively than a good manager. At the peak of an actor's career, he or she really needs someone to manage the team creating his career: to oversee the negotiation of contracts, to determine what direction is the smartest, to manage the actor's publicists, lawyers and agents, to look out for the actor's best interests, and to manage all the details.

A manager is ultimately concerned with the trajectory and long-term future of the actor's career. He or she may submit actors for projects, but also will help to initiate and maintain relationships with agents. A manager also supplies advice and guidance, as well as spending a significant amount of time and money trying to promote the talent of her clients. However, as per New York State business law, managers cannot even incidentally seek employment for an actor who is not exclusively signed to them; therefore managers do not freelance.

A manager generally takes 10-25 percent, with the most customary percentage being 15 percent. (If you are a recording artist, 20 percent is the norm.) When signed to a manager, the actor pays their manager a percentage of <u>everything</u> they earn in the entertainment industry. This can be different from an agent, who, if you are freelancing with them, only collects from gigs they helped to initiate.

There may seem to be a financial downside to having both an agent and a manager, but a good manager can do wonders for a career. Anyone really successful has both; it is always good to have as many people working to advance your career as possible.

A word of caution: Watch out for shifty agents and managers. There are certainly people trying to take advantage of actors out there. Make sure you know what you're getting into before signing with anyone. Managers are not regulated as strictly as agents, who are regulated by the state and often franchised by the unions in order to submit actors for projects—so be particularly careful with managers. If an agent or manager is legit, they will NEVER ask for any money UP FRONT, and they should be happy to provide references and examples of clients. Don't be afraid to ask questions and interview them to make sure they're a good fit.

HOW DO I GET REPRESENTATION?

This is the million-dollar question. Being unrepresented can be a big challenge. Your audition opportunities are limited, you have no one to go to for advice, and you have no one to help you make the connections you're going to need.

So how do you get an agent or a manager? It's not a simple answer. Most agents will tell you that they meet new actors:

- by attending showcases
- by teaching seminars
- through referrals, and
- sometimes from mail submissions.

These are ways to get meetings, but how do you get the agent to freelance with you or sign with you? **The answer is to create or find your own work, and once you have it, make sure you publicize it.** Continue going to open calls, continue submitting yourself online for film and commercials, continue mailing headshots and postcards, continue meeting casting directors at seminars. All of those methods will lead you to work, and booking work will help you hook an agent.

After all, an agent wants an actor who is going to make them money. Showing off your *potential* to make money is much less effective then showing them that you are *already making money*.

Another very good tactic is to use your friends. If you're in a show with an actor who has an agent, ask that actor to hook you up with a meeting. That's a very common way that actors meet agents and managers.

In research for this part of the book, we asked 50 actors how they got their agents. A couple of things surprised us, but a lot of them didn't. We'll start with the surprises.

A good number of actors—actors who would be considered successful in musical theatre—didn't have agents. They had created their careers through networking, open calls, and self-submissions. One actress bragged that she booked five national tours and never had to pay a dime to an agent. Going unrepresented can work in the musical theatre world, given the amount of EPAs and open calls available to actors. However, that does not translate to film, television and commercials where agents are critical components of any successful career.

Another thing that is surprising is how ineffective school showcases have become. When a class graduates from an acting program, they often come to New York to perform a short show to sell themselves to agents and casting directors. This is pretty standard practice for the bigger programs. In recent years—perhaps because of the economic climate—many of these events have been very poorly attended. It seemed like no one was looking for new actors. If you went to Julliard or NYU, then sure, your showcase was well attended, but not if you want to The University of South Carolina or Northwestern.

Most people I talked to say that they got their agent because they found good work themselves, and made the most of the opportunity to promote themselves. The old adage "work breeds work" is very true.

True Story from Autumn Dornfeld

(who was in *The Graduate* on Broadway)

"A few months after graduating, a director who had seen my work in college cast me in a small workshop production at The Cherry Lane downtown. One of the older actresses in the show found out I didn't have an agent and asked her own agents to make sure to come (I think this is often the best way—if you can ask a friend, preferably one who isn't your same type, to connect you with their agent). Mary Harden, owner at Harden-Curtis, came to the show and told my colleague she was interested (and that I was like a young Cynthia Nixon, which I enjoyed hearing very much, because she worked frequently in the theater when she was young). At first they just wanted to freelance, but fortunately the second audition they sent me on, for a play at Lincoln Center, I booked. So they signed me immediately, and I've been with them ever since!"

It is not always easy. You have to keep working to create your own work, to try to get agents and managers to attend, to do your mailing, to attend workshops, to strengthen your website, to network with friends…everything we're discussing in this book.

The key is to not let any opportunities slip through your fingers. If you find yourself cast in a great show, do the paperwork. Send out invitations. Collect reviews and mail them to agents. Use postcards and thank you notes thoughtfully. Every agent wants an actor who works, so keep working.

Sometimes targeting a few agents can work as well. Pick three agents and pay to meet them at a meet-and-greet seminar. Then commit to meeting them once a year for three to five years. Each year, bring them an updated list of the casting directors who know your work. Also, keep these agents up-to-date with postcards every four to six weeks. If the agent sees how much work you're putting in and how you've grown over time, you're much more likely to work together.

INDUSTRY INSIDER:

HOW DO YOU MEET NEW ACTORS AND POTENTIAL CLIENTS?

"The majority of projects these days are based on electronic submissions, so the days of filing cabinets filled with headshots are long gone. I can search actors on breakdowns, etc. I am always willing to meet new actors during castings if an agent asks me to. My goal is to know who the talent is, so I am always open to meeting if my schedule allows. I am also willing to look at reels and headshots that come from an actor's friend who might know me." —*Sean Desimone, Independent Casting Director*

"Through seminars, managers, some casting directors, pictures, and sometimes through friends and fellow performers." —*Eileen Haves, President, Eileen Haves*

Talent Agency

"We meet new actors through submissions, showcases and seminars." —*Paula Curcuru, President, PMG-Prestige Management Group*

"All sources: client/producer/casting director referrals, seeing on TV, seeing in classes, searching the web."

—*Mark Turner, Broadcast Agent, Abrams Artists Agency*

"We're very eclectic in our pursuit of new actors and potential clients. We attend showcases, workshops, Broadway, off-Broadway and regional theater. We receive recommendations from managers, entertainment attorneys, casting directors, and clients. We watch television, film and contact artists from those venues as well. In short, if it isn't illegal, immoral, or fattening, we do it!" —*Ricki Olsha, Agent, Don Buchwald*

"Generally through managers, although if I see someone in a movie or on a TV show, I go after them." —*Rachel Sheedy, Theatrical Agent, Buchwald*

"I meet new actors through headshots sent to my office, through agents/managers, and my staff going to actors' showcases." —*Don Case, President, Don Case Casting*

"Mainly from agent recommendations, and we go to see theatre often." —*Susan Gish, Casting Director, Philadelphia Casting*

THE CASTING DIRECTOR

It is an easy trap to fall into, thinking that if you sign with an agent or manager, "Ahhhh, now I can wait for them to call me with the auditions." <u>WRONG</u>. This is when you need to work even harder. You now have people working for you, and with you, on your team. Taking a proactive approach works powerfully to help an actor feel active, productive, accomplished and powerful in their career, instead of frustrated, powerless, bitter and confused.

It is easy to say, "My agent does not get me out enough," but what is actually happening is that the casting directors are not calling you in. The Casting Director (CD) is the leverage point in the business. You, therefore, need to be working the casting director angle, getting as many casting directors to know and love your work as possible. This, in turn, makes your agent's job easier and exponentially increases the odds of your success.

It can be extremely frustrating waiting for an audition to get to know a casting person, and the Catch-22 is that if the casting director does not know you, the chances of them calling you in for an audition are dramatically less—but how are casting directors supposed to know your work if they do not call you in? We want to address the following questions:

- How can you meet casting directors?

- How can you get them familiar with and confident with your work so that they are comfortable calling you in for a role?

- How can you continue to build your "fan list" of casting directors?

The answers to these questions are the key to creating your success.

INDUSTRY INSIDER:

WHAT SUGGESTIONS/TIPS DO YOU HAVE FOR ACTORS ABOUT MAKING THEM MORE REPRESENTATION-FRIENDLY?

"Be pro-active. Attend seminars, meet with casting directors, keep your Actors Access resume and your IMDB profile up-to-date. Get new pictures once a year. Get a reel and upload it to Actors Access. Create a website. Take classes at a respected acting school." —*David Rhee, Agent, Kolstein Talent*

"Don't waste our time coming to open call if you really aren't ready. You should be a completely trained actor, who can create a three-dimensional character in five minutes in the waiting room. If you've had one 'commercial' acting class or taken a few seminars, that does not make you ready to see us. An actor is trained for many years." —*Susan Gish, Casting Director, Philadelphia Casting*

"Don't nag, and be realistic about your type and character." —*Sue Schachter, Owner, Suzelle Management*

"Communicate in a quick, concise and efficient way. We tend to be very busy, so brevity is key." —*Rachel Sheedy, Theatrical Agent, Buchwald*

"Just be yourself when you walk in the room or get the call for an appointment. Everyone gets nervous and apologizes for every move they make in the room and that shows insecurity." —*Sean Desimone, Independent*

Casting Director

"Flexible, always being available when needed, low maintenance."—*Mark Turner, Broadcast Agent, Abrams Artists Agency*

"Be aware that everybody's time is precious and that an agent's to-do list is huge. Be prompt for meetings, have updated pictures, resumes, and demo reels with you, be specific in what you're looking for in an agency and be able to have an intelligent conversation about your needs, desires, and abilities. In other words, don't make the agents do the heavy lifting in the meeting." —*Ricki Olsha, Agent, Don Buchwald*

"Know who you are and what you are selling. Know what roles you're truly right for. Star quality, intelligence, personality, and great acting." —*Cyrena Esposito, Manager, Red Letter Entertainment*

"Be prepared with updated headshot/resume and reputable training." —*Paula Curcuru, President, PMG-Prestige Management Group*

"Your personality should be pleasant and outgoing but not domineering."—*Eileen Haves, President, Eileen Haves Talent Agency*

"Listen. Your audition begins upon entering my office. Fill out required material, look at the script, and ALWAYS bring your picture and resume. Cut the small talk. It's not a social event. Focus and prepare for the audition." —*Don Case, President, Don Case Casting*

Casting director workshops are often **THE MOST USEFUL, and most accessible,** tool that an actor can use. These are workshops that you pay for, and in turn you have the chance to meet, and to perform for, the casting director of your choice.

In the good old days, casting directors would schedule time out of their week to meet new actors—also known as general auditions (or generals). Some casting directors still do generals, but much less frequently than they used to. The recent trend is toward meet-and-greet seminars, where you pay a nominal fee to spend a half-hour listening to a particular agent or casting director tell you about their business and asking questions in a group of about 20 people. Then you get a five-minute one-on-one meeting with them to perform a monologue, scene or song.

There are many formats to these workshops, but the end result is the same: **For $35 to $40, you can guarantee that you and your work are seen by the person who decides who gets the audition appointments.** It is 100% more likely that you will get called in by a casting director if he/she is familiar with you and likes your work. These workshops are the best way to make them aware of you, and mailings should be used in conjunction with these workshops to reinforce the casting directors' familiarity with you.

Now, some people say, "I just don't feel comfortable paying for an audition." What we say to those people is that they should **change their mind**. It is naïve to think that you will be miraculously discovered. You must think about the industry like a business and understand how it works.

> "Happiness calls out responsive gladness in others. There is enough sadness in the world without yours. Never doubt the excellence and permanence of what is yet to be. Join the great company of those who make the barren places of life fruitful with kindness."
> — **Helen Keller**

If a Casting Director likes you, they will call you in directly, or through your agent or manager. This is how the **whole team** comes into play. It is easier for your agent or manager to submit your photo for a role if they know the casting director is familiar with your work. So all of the work you do with mailings, workshops, etc. supports the work your agent or manager is doing, by making it more likely to obtain an audition from a submission.

And of course, keep expanding the list of casting directors that know you and love your work. If you don't have an agent or manager, you can use these relationships to impress them. If you take a class with a casting director, for example Eric Woodall from Tara Rubin, and he calls you in for an audition, you can use it to market yourself. Send out a postcard the agent you want to impress and say, "I just got called in directly by Tara Rubin to audition for a show." Agents want actors with these relationships. Casting Director workshops are really useful in making your entire career move forward.

WORKING WITH YOUR REPRESENTATION

"Each client is a partnership, a conversation. You're only going to be able to go as far as they wish to go, in a way. That makes all the difference."

—Lindy Roy

This is one topic that we are uniquely qualified to discuss. A good partnership between an actor and his/her representation is crucial to maximizing potential for results. As with any relationship, communication is the key to success. Here is a list of things actors should do when working with representation:

- **Book out.** That means letting your agent/manager know ahead of time when you know you are not available to audition. He or she may be fighting to get you an audition for a day you won't even be able to make it.

- **Realize you represent the agency/company.** When you miss an appointment, arrive late, or in general, screw anything up, you're screwing it up for the agency's entire group of actors. An agent/manager becomes more powerful when they have actors that are well respected. If you miss an audition for *One Life to Live*, they might not give any more auditions to anyone your agent/manager represents.

- **Answer the phone when your agent/manager calls (or call back ASAP).** It looks good to casting people when appointments are confirmed quickly. Again, you represent every single person on the same roster. Never go more than an hour or two during the day without checking your messages. Your work day, whether you're auditioning that day or not, goes until about 6:30pm. Be available to confirm appointments.

- **Whenever possible, do not ask for appointments to be rescheduled.** It's a pain in the neck for the agent and the casting directors to have to reschedule appointments. Of course, if you have two auditions at 11am on different sides of town, then ask for a different time. But if it's at all doable then just make it work. Arrive at the first one really early and hustle to the second one. You don't want to get a reputation for being difficult by asking for time changes all the time.

- **Make sure your rep has your updated headshots with attached resumes.** These headshots should have your representative's logo on them, rather than your personal contact info. If your rep calls to ask for headshots, get them there as soon as possible.

- **Get to know your rep.** If you have a relationship with your rep, they'll know your type so much better. They'll get you more appropriate auditions and you'll book more work. A good way to do this is to volunteer to work in the office. If your rep knows you and your type, it'll make it much easier for them to get you into the right auditions. But be aware that agents and managers have BUSY schedules. Don't overstay your welcome.

- **Do your part of the job.** Meet casting directors, do mailings, send postcards, build a website, go to open calls. Do all the things we've discussed to keep your career moving forward. Don't get lazy now that you have a rep. In many cases you are earning 75-90 percent of the money, which means you need to be doing 75-90 percent of the work. YOU ARE YOUR ONLY CLIENT.

- **Never say disparaging things about your agent/manager or a casting director to another agent/manager or casting director.** It is a very small business and it will get back to them.

- **If something is not working, schedule a time to talk to your agent/manager and do the research to determine what is missing and what would make a difference.** For example, if you are not getting a lot of auditions, research whether there are projects happening that are right for you, and research whether or not you have been submitted for those projects. If you have been submitted and are not getting the appointments, look to see if you have done what you need to do to meet that casting director. Maybe you should schedule a workshop to meet them.

- **Set goals with your rep.** Periodically, it's a great idea to sit down with your rep and set some goals. From the actor's perspective, you can ask the rep what you can be doing to make their job easier: who you should meet, what classes will strengthen your resume, what kind of promotion should you be doing for yourself. From the rep's perspective, they'll get an idea of what you really want out of your relationship and out of your career.

- **Keep a list of your goals handy.** Print it them out, and keep them where you can see them, and they can motivate you. Send a copy to your rep, so they can keep you accountable and working toward them. It's really hard to reach your goals if you don't know what they are.

AUDITIONING AND FEEDBACK

> "I'll do my dreaming with my eyes wide open, and I'll do my looking back with my eyes closed."
>
> **—Tony Arata**

If you have an audition, that day some of your energy will be spent in figuring out where you are going, how to get there, what to wear, and in getting prepared for the actual audition. Surprisingly enough, this period can often be a stressful time for both actor and representation, particularly if an actor is juggling their auditions with their other work schedule.

Arriving on time, making sure your have the right headshot (**always** bring your headshot and resume to an audition, even if you know they already have one) and other factors frequently take more time than you might imagine, so the most prepared actors build in extra time for unforeseen contingencies. Once you are in the audition, concentrating solely on your acting performance is sometimes easier said than done.

Since you only have five to ten minutes with the casting director (if that), many actors put an extraordinary effort in trying to glean additional information from them. This is not always productive. Certainly you can ask a question or two about the scene, but asking a lot questions to try and gauge their thoughts on your performance usually makes you appear inexperienced and ill prepared. Ask something if you truly need to know, but they want to see YOU. They want to see *your* choices. Anyone can read the lines. What are you bringing to the piece that is distinctly you? This is all a casting director wants.

INDUSTRY INSIDER: WHAT IS THE NUMBER ONE TURN-OFF AN ACTOR CAN DO IN A MEETING/AUDITION?

"No-nos include being late, unprepared, and inappropriately dressed (if you wear it to a barbecue, don't wear it to a meeting)." —*Ricki Olsha, Agent, Don Buchwald*

"Being boring or over-selling themselves."—*Mark Turner, Broadcast Agent, Abrams Artists Agency*

"Showing desperation." —*Cyrena Esposito, Manager, Red Letter Entertainment*

"Being late for an interview, not being able to tell the agent what their interests and needs are." —*Eileen Haves, President, Eileen Haves Talent Agency*

"Chewing Gum." —*Paula Curcuru, President, PMG-Prestige Management Group*

"Being arrogant about his or her career." —*Sue Schachter, Owner, Suzelle Management*

"Here's a number of my 'number one' turn offs: One, male actors who come unshaven (unless specified for the role). Two, men/women who come looking like the just rolled out of bed with dirty hair, etc. Three, actors who barely read the script, are not even looking at stage directions, or who are socializing with other actors. Four, actors who phone/email. Five, actors who

can't see the board in studio but won't or don't use glasses or contacts. Six, actors who are not prepared."
—*Don Case, President, Don Case Casting*

"Complaining about or bad-mouthing people they've worked with in the past." —*Rachel Sheedy, Theatrical Agent, Buchwald*

"Being late. Telling me they didn't know the shoot date. Talking badly about the script or similar." —*Susan Gish, Casting Director, Philadelphia Casting*

"Don't ask me what the next step is. I am on your side. I called you in for a reason, so just let me submit you and wait for notes from my client." —*Sean Desimone, Independent Casting Director*

Post audition, many actors' concerns revolve around second-guessing themselves. What did I do right versus wrong? Did they like me? What could I have done differently?

While these are all great questions to review after each audition, many actors make the mistake of continually spinning over and over on these concerns. It is no wonder that these actors will eventually find the audition process frustrating. The bottom line is that the most feedback you will get is booking the job or getting a callback. Beyond that, you will waste a lot of time and energy focusing on whether you were right for the part and continually replaying the audition over in your head.

Many actors call their agent or manager and ask for feedback. Although feedback is something actors desperately want, it is usually the last thing a casting director wants to give. Don't count on feedback. If you get it, great, but for the most part the feedback is that if you do not get a callback, you were not right for the role. This does not even mean you did a good or bad job, necessarily, simply that you did not get a callback.

A casting director sees scores of people for a particular role. Don't ask for feedback unless it is offered. It can be quite annoying to the casting director, which of course is not helpful to you or your representative. Think of feedback as the 'F' word. See if you can eliminate it from your mental and verbal vocabulary.

The point here is: if you think you did a really good job and you did not get a callback, then *maybe* ask for feedback, sparingly. Also, if you got a callback and did not book, it can be useful to find out why. In all other cases, move on to the next audition. Get feedback from your acting teacher. Do not rely on it from casting directors. They are busy and rarely remember how a specific actor did, unless they were either horrible or amazing.

True Story from Guy

A wise director I once worked with, Shorey Walker, who is also a well-established performer herself, told me, "Auditioning is your job; working is your vacation." That always stuck with me. When you think of it like that, it changes the way you look at your career.

Auditioning is hard work, and it deserves all of your focus. When you've walked out of the room and you know you've given a great audition, your work is done. Feel proud of that. Even if you didn't book the gig, you've laid the groundwork for you getting the next one.

If you get the call that you booked the gig, that's amazing. You get to act! You get the opportunity to do

> what you came to New York to do. That doesn't sound
> like work to me; it sounds like fun.

Whether your team includes an agent and a
manager or your team is just you, the main idea
remains the same: Behave professionally, study your
craft, meet the casting directors you need to know,
follow up, stay focused, grateful and respectful, and
you are well on your way.

Chapter 8: The Boring Stuff

This wouldn't be a very helpful "how-to" book if it didn't discuss the less glamorous but crucial aspects of acting in New York: namely, the unions and tax information.

The Unions are ultimately there to protect actors and, though it gets complicated, most do just that. As far as taxes go, actors are lucky! They can deduct many expenses that people in other jobs can't. Also in this section are some programs that are exclusively for artists, and which can be a major help.

THE UNIONS

There are three major unions that most New York actors deal with: Actors Equity Association (also known as "Equity" or AEA), Screen Actors Guild (SAG), and The American Federation of Television and Radio Artists (AFTRA). These three unions don't really function in the way most American unions function. A plumber's union will provide training, certification, job placement, and finally, protect of a plumber's rights on the job. For the most part, Equity, SAG and AFTRA do only the last part. The membership of these unions outnumbers the jobs available by such a large degree that they can do very little to help actors get work. Most of their time and money is spent ensuring that the available jobs pay well, and that the conditions are such that they allow actors to do their best work.

Actors Equity Association

As New York is a theatre city, let's begin with Equity. Actors Equity Association (AEA) is the union that represents actors in theatrical productions. All Broadway shows operate under Equity contracts, as do the large majority of Off-Broadway shows. Additionally, Equity has a plethora of contacts, in New York and all over the United States, each with its own set of requirements and pay scale: Production Contracts, Touring Contracts, Theatre for Young Audiences, Cabaret, LORT, COST, and CORST, to name a few.

Working under an Equity contract offers an actor a lot of benefits. Equity protects actors from being overworked, requiring that a strict break schedule is upheld. If an actor misses a break for some reason, the producers have to pay the actor a penalty. There are other protections as well, including a limit on the number of performances, a limit on the amount of rehearsal, specifications about the conditions under which work is done—everything, all the way down to the tiniest details. Most Equity contracts require there to be a daybed available to actors who want to take a nap!

Health insurance and pension are the other two primary benefits of working under Equity contracts. However, in order to qualify for Health and Pension, you have to work a certain number of weeks per year. Currently, you have to have 12 weeks of employment within a year to qualify for six months of insurance, and one-half of a pension credit. In order to get a full pension credit and a full year's insurance, you have to work 20 weeks. Very few members of Equity can find enough work during a year to qualify—probably less than two percent at any given time.

There are several ways to get your Equity card. The first one is to get an Equity job. It sounds simple enough, but it can actually be quite difficult. In a lot of cases, non-union actors can't even get seen for Equity gigs. There are thousands of Union actors and only so many jobs.

One tactic for non-union actors to score a union gig is to crash EPAs. EPAs are Equity Principal Auditions. They are the open call auditions that every Equity show is required to have. This gives Equity actors a chance to be seen for every big project out there. If there is extra time, casting directors will often allow non-union actors to audition as well. There are no guarantees of this, and it can be a huge waste of time, but some people get their card this way.

There is also the EMC program. A non-union actor can work at a participating theatre as an Equity Membership Candidate. After 50 weeks are accrued, the actor can join. Very few people join this way, but for some it's a good option.

An actor can join Equity by being a member of a sister union (i.e. AFTRA, SAG, AGVA, AGMA, GIAA). You have to have been a member for at least one year, and you have to be in good standing. Additionally, you'd have to have worked under a principal or "under-five" contract, or have worked as an extra at least three times. (See glossary for definitions of terms.)

There is a special loophole unique to New York: you can get your Equity card by booking a gig with one of the touring children's theatre companies. Several of the big children's theatre touring companies, TheatreWorks USA being the biggest, love to cast non-equity actors. This allows the actors to join the union. They operate under a Theatre for Young Audiences (TYA) contract, which can be grueling. These are hard jobs, but they pay, they provide insurance and pension weeks, and you can get your card. It's a popular way to go. TYA companies have regular open calls. Check

Backstage and ActorsEquity.org for opportunities.

The current fee for joining Actors Equity is $1100, and you can arrange to pay over time. Annual dues are $118, and actors must pay 2.25% of their gross amount of paychecks from Equity jobs.

When Should I Join AEA?

The decision to join Equity is a really big moment in a New York actor's life. It can be an agonizing decision.

Once you join Equity, you are no longer allowed to do non-union work, which cuts you off from a ton of opportunity. If you leaf through *Backstage* you'll see there are dozens of shows casting each month, ranging from tiny summer stock theatres to exciting and prestigious national tours. Non-union shows are a great way to build a resume and sharpen your skills, but the conditions and the pay are usually not very good. There are exceptions of course—some of the national tours pay over $1000 per week, and the actors are treated incredibly well—but the large majority are not ideal gigs.

Once you join Equity, every job you work will have to meet or exceed the minimum salary standard Equity has very clearly defined. You will have your breaks, your time will be well managed, and you will have comfortable lodging. Most importantly, you will be paid well, and you'll get insurance and pension weeks.

Equity members also get the right to audition at any EPA or Chorus Call. They can't always see every actor that attends, but they do a really good job of seeing as many as possible. Every show has these open calls, and every long-running show has required calls twice a year.

There are other perks. The bathroom at Actors Equity on 46th St. is one of the cleanest you'll find in New York. There are free and discounted tickets for members to see shows. And you get the prestige of putting a tiny AEA next to your name on your resume. Not bad!

Screen Actors Guild

Screen Actors Guild (SAG) is the largest actors' union. SAG contracts cover actors in film, on television, in commercials, and on the Internet. According to the SAG website, their mission is three-fold: to preserve and expand work opportunities, to negotiate and enforce fair contracts, and to collect the proper compensation.

When you work under a SAG contract, you are generally treated well and compensated well. An actor receives a "day-rate" for each day or partial day of filming, plus residuals. Residuals are the payments an actor receives for every time the work is shown. The pay scale for residuals is incredibly complicated. Rates change based on how many times the piece is shown, in what markets, at what time of the day, and a variety of factors. Luckily, SAG is really diligent about tracking residuals. Additionally, for some projects you can log on to the SAG website and track your own residuals.

Much like there is Equity and non-Equity theatre, there are SAG and non-SAG films and commercials. Of course SAG covers big budget films, most primetime television (though some is covered by AFTRA), and most of the commercials you see on television. But, in New York, non-union actors can find a ton of opportunity is non-union film and in the non-union commercial market. Once an actor joins SAG, he is no longer allowed to work on non-union projects.

There are three ways to join SAG. First, you can book a principal or speaking role in a SAG project. Second, you can join through a sister union, if you've been a member for over a year, and have worked as a principal in that union. The third way is through doing SAG background (extra) work. Most big SAG projects employ both SAG and non-SAG background players. If you are hired as non-SAG background or get upgraded to SAG background, you receive what is known as a "waiver." After three waivers, you can join SAG.

Joining SAG is pricey! The initiation fee is $2,277. The yearly dues are $116, and actors working under SAG contracts must pay the union a percentage of their gross out of each paycheck. This percentage varies, depending on how much you earned that year, from .25 percent to 1.85 percent. SAG does not accept personal checks for the initiation, and it must all be paid at the time of joining; there is no payment plan.

When Should I Join SAG?

The answer to this question in LA is as soon as possible! In the LA market, where film and television are the focus, an actor is invisible until he has his SAG card. In New York, a lot of people feel the same way, but don't be so quick to join. In fact, the best advice is: don't join SAG until you have to.

There has been a shift in New York toward more and more non-union work, especially in the commercial world. About 80 percent of all of the commercials and voice-overs in country are cast in New York. No statistics are available on this particular issue, but it seems that about half of them are non-union. Non-union commercial contracts are usually "buy-outs", meaning the actor receives one lump payment for the use of his image, with no residuals.

Payments range from $100 to $100,000, but most contracts sit in the $1,000 to $3,000 range.

A New York actor who is SAG, but who doesn't have a powerful commercial agent, may find himself not getting very many auditions. Since there is so much money in commercials, the auditions are very sought after. If an actor doesn't have a well-known and influential agent, he may not be able to even get in the door. There is plenty of opportunity for a non-union actor in the commercial market. An agent who can get you non-union auditions is fairly easy to obtain.

Even though the money is much less, there is a lot to be gained by doing non-union commercials. They give the actor a chance to sharpen his skills, and get some commercials under his belt, all in a much less competitive talent pool. Additionally, the casting directors that cast non-union commercials are very often the same ones that cast the lucrative union commercials. Each non-union audition helps build a relationship with the casting director, and it's these relationships that create longevity in the industry.

An actor is allowed to work three SAG jobs before joining SAG. Before the fourth, the actor must pay up, or he or she won't be allowed on set. This is called being a "must join." In order to qualify for health insurance, an actor must either work 74 days or earn $14,350 under SAG contracts. An actor earning over $15,000 is a year will qualify for a pension credit.

In LA, there is more of a stigma attached to not being SAG. It makes the actor seem amateur and in some cases, untouchable. In New York there is virtually no stigma. Casting directors in film and television are more than happy to audition non-union actors.

The American Federation of Television and Radio Artists

The distinction between SAG and AFTRA, The American Federation of Television and Radio Artists, is slight, and getting less distinct all the time. The rule of thumb is that SAG covers projects on film, and AFTRA covers projects on tape. With the advent and prevalence of digital media, things can get confusing. AFTRA covers television news, syndicated television, audio recordings, radio commercials, game shows, reality shows, soaps, and talk shows. A few prime-time television shows are also AFTRA: *Gossip Girl*, *Damages*, and *Rescue Me*, to name a few.

Anyone can join AFTRA. You can even do it online. If you pony up the initiation fee, they will send you a card. There isn't much non-union AFTRA-type work. If an actor works one day on an AFTRA project, he has 30 days to officially join if he ever wants to work again. For example, if the casting director for *Saturday Night Live* asks an actress to do a day of extra work on October 1st, she's free to do it without joining. During the next 30 days, she can work at *Saturday Night Live* or any other AFTRA project. After October 31st, she will not be allowed on any AFTRA set without a membership. This is strictly enforced. AFTRA representatives have been known to show up on set and ask for a credit card.

The initiation fee is $1,300 and the minimum dues are $127.80 per year. To qualify for insurance under AFTRA, you must earn $10,000 but less than $30,000 in four consecutive quarters or less. Earn $7,500, and you'll get one year's pension credit.

When Should I Join AFTRA?

Generally there is no need to join AFTRA until you have to. There's no stigma to being non-AFTRA among most casting directors. However, if you want to do extra work (which can be fun and lucrative) you're more likely to be called if you're AFTRA or have made it clear that you're willing to join.

If you're eager to be a member of SAG or Equity, you can try to get in through the back door as an AFTRA member. If you're an AFTRA member for over year, and you've worked in any principal or "under-five" role, or have done three background jobs, you can join SAG or Equity.

Financial Core

Deciding whether or not to join the unions is a critical decision in an actor's career, and we've outlined some of the things to think about before joining. Joining the unions may limit the work you can do.

There is one loophole, however, with SAG. An actor can become "financial core." When this happens, he can work for any rate that he thinks is fair—that includes non-union work.

Sounds too good to be true, right? Well, there are some drawbacks. A financial core (Fi-Core) member of SAG is referred to as a "fee paying non-member," so he loses some of the rights that SAG members have.

Some of the rights you lose when you declare financial core are:

• The right to vote in SAG elections

- The right to hold SAG office

- The right to use iActor, a web service run by SAG

- The right to represent yourself as SAG on your resume or on the Internet

- The right to call yourself a member of SAG or have a SAG card

- The right to re-join SAG without a formal hearing and without repaying the initiation fee

Some of the rights you gain:

- The right to work on non-union projects

- The continued right to work on SAG projects

- The right to pension and health if you qualify under SAG rules

In order to become Fi-Core with SAG, you must first join SAG. You pay your initiation fee, and start paying your dues. (Even after you turn in your card, you still have to pay your dues and fees. Your dues will be 5-10 percent less, however.) Pension and health is completely separate from the SAG office. Don't worry about losing those benefits.

If you make the decision to become Fi-Core, you have to call SAG, and they will walk you through the steps. SAG desperately wants you NOT to go Fi-Core. In fact, there is someone at each office designated to try to talk you out of it. And their arguments are compelling. They will tell you that SAG does everything it can to keep conditions high and pay high, through collective bargaining. They will tell you that SAG has a rich history, which you will no longer be a part of. They will tell you that Fi-Core SAG members are seen as scabs and anti-union by the industry at large.

The argument for the other side is quite compelling as well. Why limit yourself to work that is SAG-approved? If you are making money, or potentially could make money doing non-union gigs, why shouldn't you? Can't the actor decide for himself what he's willing to work for?

Additionally, from a marketing standpoint, if you become a SAG member with a weak resume, and limited relationships in the industry, you may be sunk. Even if you *have* a strong agent, you may only get a few auditions a month. If you can take SAG and non-SAG auditions, you could have 20 or 40 auditions per month. Also, the best way to get a powerful agent is to book work and let everyone know that you're booking work. Your chances of booking work are much higher if you can audition for everything.

The real truth of the commercial market in New York is that non-union commercials are plentiful, and they are here to stay. The very same casting directors that cast the incredibly lucrative SAG commercials often cast non-union commercials. If you come in to audition for small non-SAG commercials and do a great job (maybe even book a few), of course the casting directors will start calling you in for SAG jobs. Then you can tell all of the top agents that you have this great relationship with a casting director, and that's how you get the great agents. That's just an example, but the point is: why cut yourself off from money and connections?

It should be noted that in Los Angeles, there is more of a stigma to being Fi-Core. Many actors who are Fi-Core keep it under wraps in New York. However, with only a few exceptions, no one really cares.

This is and should be a tough decision, so consider carefully.

GOVERNMENT ASSISTANCE

It may sound weird to think about using government assistance, but we'd like to point out a few programs that might help an actor financially connect the dots. You can find information about all of these programs at www.NYC.gov or by calling 311 from your phone.

- **Unemployment Insurance.** We all pay the government for unemployment insurance, every time we earn anything. That money is set aside for when we find ourselves without work. There is no shame in taking that money back.

- **Food Stamps.** Food stamps are government subsidies for food and other grocery items that people require to live. Many actors have used food stamps. If you find yourself under a certain level of income, you are entitled to them.

- **Subsidized Housing.** Programs like 80/20 housing, Mitchell Lama, and Common Ground are provided by the city, and sometimes by private companies, to help low-income people find affordable places to live. In the 80/20 program for instance, people with incomes under a certain limit can get apartments in luxury buildings for a fraction of the market value rent. (The Actors Fund has a really comprehensive seminar on how to apply for these apartments.)

- **Medicaid.** Most of us know how scary it can be to be without insurance. Medicaid provides basic medical services at affordable rates for low-income people. If you qualify, get a Medicaid card. It could save you a financial catastrophe in the event of a medical emergency.

In some cases, the only way actors have been able to stay in the business is by taking advantage of these programs from time to time. Do your research and find out what you're entitled to.

TAXES: THE GOOD NEWS AND THE BAD NEWS

The good news is: you are making money as an actor. The bad news is: you are making money as an actor. If you are making money, then the government wants its share.

Warning: this section is very detailed and only interesting and useful if you are dealing with your expenses for tax purposes, so feel free to skip ahead if this is not immediately necessary for you.

Because the tax deductions are reported on two different tax forms, with professional income reported on both form W-2 (most union income and television, film and commercials) and form 1099 (most non-union work and some print jobs), it's going to get complicated quickly.

What is a Deductible Expense?

According to the IRS, all deductible business expenses:

- Are those that are incurred in connection with your trade, business, or profession
- Must be "ordinary" and "necessary"
- Must "NOT be lavish or extravagant under the circumstances"

For a performer certain basic expenses easily fit the above criteria: travel (which includes hotel and meals—only 50 percent deductible—etc.), vehicle and transportation, equipment, supplies, wardrobe, home office expenses, legal and professional fees, video costs, agent fees, manager fees, promotional expenses, etc. We'll review some of the more complex and contentious deduction areas, but first let's discuss income.

Income for the Performer

Actors, singers, dancers and other performers face some challenges when trying to prepare their tax returns. Irregular payments, unusual business-related expenses, and supplemental income in the form of "regular" jobs all add up to a more complicated than average tax return. Many artists end up with a combination of income types: income from regular wages and income from self-employment.

Income from wages involves a regular paycheck with all appropriate taxes, social security and Medicare withheld. Income from self-employment may be in the form of cash, check, or goods, with no withholding of any kind. The business-related expenses are deducted differently for each type of income, and you will need to complete several different forms in order to do so. Review the guidelines below to determine the correct way to deduct your expenses.

If You Get a Regular Paycheck

If you've got a gig lasting more than a few weeks, chances are you will get paid regular wages with all taxes withheld. At the end of the year, your employer will issue you a W-2 form. If this regular paycheck is for entertainment-related work (and not just for waiting tables to keep the rent paid), you will deduct related expenses on a Schedule A, under "Unreimbursed Employee Business Expenses," or on Form 2106, which will give you a total to carry to the Schedule A. The type of expenses that go here are:

- Union dues.
- Apparel: Uniforms, costumes, special shoes (tap, ballet, character, or anything else not suitable for street wear), theatrical makeup, and wigs.
- Cleaning of work-related apparel.
- Education: Acting, voice, or dance lessons, or other education related to improving or maintaining your performance skills.
- Photographs, videos, or CDs used for self-promotion and marketing.

Income for the performer is: all payments for performances, guest appearances, income from teaching, voiceover work, film and video work, directing, choreography, etc. regardless of whether you receive a 1099 or W-2 at year's end.

It is a common misconception that if you do not get tax forms at year's end then it is not reportable income. This is untrue. If you have income in any form (including barters and free products from endorsements), it is required to be reported on your 1040. The form 1099-MISC tax form is supposed to be filed on any payments made to an individual for services amounting to more than $600 in any calendar year. When you are paid as an employee on a W-2, the employer withholds federal, state and local (if applicable) income tax as well as the FICA taxes, Social Security and Medicare.

If You Are Considered an Independent Contractor

Independent contractors get paid by cash or check with no withholding of any kind. This means that you are responsible for all of the Social Security and Medicare normally paid or withheld by your employer; this is called Self-Employment Tax. In order to take your deductions, you will need to complete a Schedule C, which breaks down expenses into even more detail. In addition to the items listed above, you will probably have items in the following categories:

- **Advertising**: Promotional and marketing materials go here, as do any ads you place offering your services.

- **Legal and professional fees**: Commissions to agents, attorney fees, and tax preparation fees go here. You can also put union dues here if the membership is not tied to any one job.

- **Auto/transportation expenses**: Track your mileage to auditions, keep receipts for the bus or subway, and hang on to plane and train ticket info.

- **Insurance**: Any special insurance or bond required because of your work. NOTE: Health insurance is deducted elsewhere, so don't include it here.

- **Supplies**: Shoes, costumes, makeup and office supplies go here.

- **Other**: Postage, cell phone if devoted exclusively to work, fax or photocopy fees, classes, reference materials, subscriptions, and anything else related to getting or performing work. If in doubt, keep the receipt, note what it was for, and ask your accountant or the IRS.

If You Have a Combination of Income Types

You will be better off subtracting as many expenses as you can on the Schedule C, since this will lower your Self Employment Tax. If an expense relates to both types, either put it all on the C or break it down and put a percentage on the C. Don't lie, but take the time to figure out what can legitimately be deducted against each type of income.

If all of this seems overwhelming or confusing, go to a professional tax preparer. The most important thing for you to do is keep track of your income and expenses. You can always pay someone to put everything in the right place on the right form for you, but good record keeping is crucial. Don't forget to keep your receipts!

SAMPLE LIST OF POSSIBLE TAX-DEDUCTIBLE EXPENSES

ADVERTISING & PUBLICITY
- Business Cards, Stationery, Postcards, etc
- Business Gifts
- Demo (tape, CD, DVD, audio, video)
- Photo Shoots, Reproductions, Lithos, etc.
- Resume Service & Reproduction
- Web Site, Domain, Web Hosting, etc.
- Publicist Fees

- Misc./Other

BUSINESS MEALS / ENTERTAINMENT (in town)
- Business Meals
- Entertainment for Business

BUSINESS FINANCE
- Business Bank Fees Paid
- Business Interest Paid
- Misc. / Other

COMMISSIONS & FEES
- Agent
- Manager
- Other

OFFICE EXPENSE
- Batteries
- Copy Service
- Fax Service
- Office Supplies
- Postage, Freight, Courier
- Printer Supplies (ink, paper, toner, etc.)
- Misc. / Other

CONTRACT LABOR
- Accompanist
- Writer / Producer
- Misc. / Other

PROFESSIONAL FEES (SERVICES)
- Attorney, Legal Fees (Business)
- Bookkeeper / Accountant (Business)
- Royalties Paid
- Professional Registries (i.e., players directory, casting services, call service)
- Sides
- Misc. / Other

EQUIPMENT PURCHASE
- Type:

OUT OF TOWN TRAVEL
- Fare:
- Where:
- Purpose:

LODGING
- Car Rental, Taxi, Subway, Bus, Parking and Tolls
- Meals and Incidental Expenses

I DON'T UNDERSTAND WHY "CAR RENTAL, ETC.
GOES UNDER "LODGING"

UTILITIES (not for home or office)
- Cable / Satellite
- Communications (phone/fax/cell/pager/voicemail/phone card)
- ISP (Internet Service Provider)
- Misc. / Other

REPAIRS / MAINTENANCE
- Costume Repair / Cleaning / Maintenance
- Equipment
- Instrument Tuning (i.e., piano)
- Professional Tools
- Misc. / Other

SUPPLIES
- Books, Scripts, Music
- Uniforms, Professional Costumes, Software
- Props
- Misc. / Other

LICENSES
- Licenses (i.e., city business license, professional, etc.)
- Misc. / Other

OTHER
- Dues: Professional Services, Societies, Organizations, Theatre Companies
- Dues: Union

MISCELLANEOUS
- Charity Cash / Check / Mileage & Parking (for charity)
- Charity Other (goods)
- Medical / Dental / Vision

- Medical Insurance Premiums
- Medical Mileage & Parking
- Student Loan Interest

For more information, we recommend purchasing *The New Tax Guide for Artists of Every Persuasion*, which is where most of this tax information has been taken from; the book contains more information as well as dozens of real life tax situations for the performer. We also suggest visiting http://www.howtodothings.com/finance-and-money/a2779-how-to-take-tax-deductions-for-actors-and-entertainers.html, which is another great resource and a place where you can download tracking sheets for tax purposes.

We emphasize that you should review your taxes with a tax professional before filing your taxes. When you are shopping for a tax preparer, please make sure they have some experience in taxation for performers.

Volunteer Income Tax Assistance (VITA)

If you are a paid-up member of Equity, AFTRA or SAG, you can have someone from the VITA office help you with your taxes. They have a very well-trained volunteer staff that can prepare your taxes for you, free of charge. Actor's taxes can be very complicated, and these volunteers know all the ins-and-outs of your return.

There is one day a year when most of the appointments are made, the first Monday in February. Go to the website for the union you belong to, and search VITA. Find out where and when you have to get on line to secure your appointment. It's not very well publicized, so search it out.

You wait on line, you make an appointment for another day, and you come back. That day you arrive with your worksheets filled out, and with all the required documents, and you leave with your returns completely done.

A word of advice: the volunteers at VITA are very concerned about keeping their funding and not getting into trouble. They will not lie for you on your returns. Often when you pay an accountant $500 to work on your return, he'll be willing to fudge some details, but not at VITA. They are on the up-and-up.

***

THE ACTORS FUND

> "The race of mankind would perish did they cease to aid each other. We cannot exist without mutual help. All therefore that need aid have a right to ask it from their fellow men; and no one who has the power of granting can refuse it without guilt."
> **—Sir Walter Scott**

The Actors Fund is a wonderful resource and a great organization that provides amazing, free services to actors. All of their information is available at www.actorsfund.org.

In some cases you have to prove that you're an actor to take part in their seminars, either by showing your union cards, or documenting your work in the field. That can be done with pay stubs, or even posters and programs. They will work with you; they really are there to help actors.

I mentioned computer classes, but there are so many more classes and seminars: getting affordable health insurance, finding an income-generating job, securing affordable housing, networking, and the list goes on.

They have programs for elderly actors, disabled actors, sick actors, dancers, and young performers. If you find yourself surprised by a financial burden, they offer financial assistance. They even have a Shoe Fund. Once a year actors can get a free pair of shoes, as long as they fill out the online form and mail it back with the receipt.

Also check out The Al Hirschfeld clinic, which operates under the auspices of The Actors Fund. They provide services, including prescriptions, referrals, and even rehabilitation if you are injured, to performers without health insurance. They are some of the nicest medical professionals in New York! They are by appointment only.

This Actors Fund is such a huge help, and it really lends support. What a great organization!

Conclusion: Good Luck and Godspeed

> "If one advances confidently in the direction of his dreams and endeavors to live the life which he has imagined, he will meet with success unexpected in common hours."
>
> **—Henry David Thoreau**

NOW WHAT?

In the preceding chapters you have gotten everything you will need to know to design a comprehensive marketing plan for your career. Start with your basic tools: your headshot, your resume and your audition material. Develop a mailing system that both makes sense to you and is sustainable. Incorporate some of the intermediate tools: your website, your reel and your voiceover demo. Pair all that with some introspection about *why* you want to be an actor. Figure out where the desire comes from, and make sure that you're living the dream every day, rather than chasing it and never quite catching it. This dual philosophy is the smartest, most efficient and most satisfying way to *make it*—and to create a fulfilling career while paying your rent.

> "All our dreams can come true, if we have the courage to pursue them."
> **—Walt Disney**

Now the real work begins. One habit common to most of the successful actors we know is setting goals, and then, naturally, working towards those goals. At this point, go back to the earlier chapters and figure out your goals. Do you need to find a photographer?

Do you need to start sending Thank You cards on a regular basis? Do you need to meet the casting directors of *Law and Order*? Do you need to reconnect with your childhood passion for performing? Do you need to figure out exactly what your DreamSource is and remind yourself of it every day?

> "The best way to make your dreams come true is to wake up."
> **—Paul Valery**

Make a list of the steps you're going to take to fast-track your career. Don't over-commit yourself. Take some time to prioritize and really weigh out how much time, money and effort (both physical and emotional) you're willing to commit to the process.

It helps to divide your goals into short-term and long-term goals. For your short-term goals (e.g. Step 1: Complete all of the DreamSource exercises. Step 2: Do a targeted mailing to commercial agents.), give yourself deadlines. Be specific. For the long-term goals (eg. Book a national commercial. Act in a Broadway play.), deadlines may not be realistic. But having a list of the things you want to accomplish is vital! You can't get any work done until you know what you're working toward.

Once you have these goals set, write them down, sign them and give them to a friend or colleague who will hold you accountable. You need someone who won't let you slide, who will call you on May 1st and ask, "Have you registered for an improv class yet?!"

> "The future belongs to those who believe in the beauty of their dreams."
>
> **—Eleanor Roosevelt**

We guarantee that once you have a solid plan and you understand that where you are in your career is exactly where you need to be, your life will change dramatically. Imagine the relief you'll feel when you know you're controlling every factor that is within your power to control. Imagine the satisfaction you'll feel when you're no longer chasing your dream; you're living your dream. Imagine what you can accomplish when you're present, focused, confident, and living exactly the life you want to be living.

The next time someone says to you, "I hear you're an aspiring actor," reply with confidence, "No, I am an IN-spiring actor."

> "So many of our dreams at first seem immobile, then they seem improbable, and then, when we summon the will, they soon become inevitable."
>
> **—Christopher Reeve**

Glossary

There is a lot of jargon in the entertainment business and it helps to know what everything means, therefore we are including a summary of some frequently used terms so you can better equip yourself to speak "Actor."

DICTIONARY OF TERMS

Actor Slate – Breakdown Services, the website through which many auditions are set, offers actors a chance to pay to put themselves on film. It's basically an interview that they cut together and upload to your profile on the website. It's not as good as having a reel on there, but it's a great first step.

AEA – AEA is the short way of saying Actors Equity Association, the union for stage productions.

AFTRA – AFTRA is short for The American Federation of Television and Radio Artists, the union for taped medium.

Audition – The opportunity to interview for a role, or try out for a part.

AD – Assistant Director. The person who helps the filmmaker in the making of a movie or television show. The duties of an AD include setting the shooting schedule, tracking daily progress against the filming production schedule, arranging logistics, preparing daily call sheets, checking the arrival of cast and crew, maintaining order on the set, rehearsing cast, and directing extras.

Background – See Extra work

Book – A selection of songs that you are able to (and

comfortable with) performing at a moment's notice. Your book is often a three-ring binder with marked sheet music.

Booking – Firm commitment to a performer to do a specific job.

Breakdown – There are two kinds of breakdowns, production breakdowns and casting breakdowns:

Production Breakdowns are a summary/description of a script prepared by or for the casting director often including the names of the director, producer, network or studio, together with audition location and times, storyline and roles available for casting in a production. These are, and have traditionally been, provided only to qualified talent agents. Production breakdowns are posted on the Casting Workbook by the Casting Director and go out to as many as 1000 agents in 20 cities.

Casting Breakdowns are a list of the attributes desired in an actor, for a role to be cast. They will often include things like age, race (if that's important), and other physical characteristics, but also less tangible qualities like: funny, sardonic, powerful presence.

Buyout – A buyout is the money paid to an actor for the use of a piece of material for a certain amount of time. As opposed to residual payment, where an actor gets money each time the piece is used, a buyout is one lump sum for the unlimited use of that material, for the term of the contract.

Callback – The second audition or follow-up interview, after an initial audition.

Call Sheet – Sheet containing the cast and crew call times for a specific day's shooting. Scene numbers, the expected day's total pages, locations, and production needs are also included.

Call Time – Actual time an actor is due on the set.

Cheat – Actor's adjustment of body position away from what might be absolutely "natural" in order to accommodate the camera; can also mean looking in a different place from where the other actor actually is.

Casting Assistant – Auditions are often hectic, and a casting assistant helps the casting director make things run smoothly at auditions. They will often take digital pictures, and organize the lists. Casting assistants often become casting directors. It's important to treat them with respect.

Casting Director – To simply state it, a Casting Director is a person who matches the right actor to the roles available. The Casting Director schedules auditions for actors, through their representation, and/or by directly contacting actors. They preside over the auditions and help narrow down the choices for the director and producer who make the final decisions.

Cold Reading – A cold reading is a type of audition where the actor receives the material on the spot. He has little time or no time to prepare it and must give his best performance.

Comp Card – A composite card is a tool used mostly in modeling and print. It's like a headshot, but it's printed on 8.5"x5.5" card stock, instead of 8"x10" and contains several pictures of the model in different looks.

Contract Role – Typically a term used for soap operas for actors that have a guaranteed number of episodes per week by contract.

Copy – Script for a commercial or voiceover.

Co-Star – A role where an actor has more than five lines but is credited at the end of the show versus the opening credits.

Day Out of Days – This is the schedule for a film project that shows which actors are working on which days in which locations.

Day Player (Day Performer) – A principal performer hired on a daily basis, rather than on a longer-term contract.

Demo Reel – A sample of an actor's performances. Film/Acting Demos are usually under five minutes, and contained edited clips of the actor performing, usually from film and television, but also from stage productions, classes and home video. A Voiceover Demo is an audio recording of an actor's voice, usually doing bits of commercials. Other kinds of demos include: Commercial, Hosting, Green Screen, Animation Voices and Audiobook/Books-on-Tape.

Director – A person who directs the making of a film, television show, commercial or play. A director visualizes the script, controlling a project's artistic and dramatic aspects, while guiding the technical crew and actors in the fulfillment of his or her vision.

Director of Photography (DP) – The person who supervises all decisions regarding lighting, camera lenses, color and filters, camera angle set-ups, camera crew and film processing.

Equity – The short way of saying Actors Equity Association, the union for stage productions.

Extra Work – Most film and television productions need actors to stand in the background of their shots from time to time. This is called extra work. The pay varies, but doing extra work is a great way to get used to the goings-on on a big set.

Financial Core – A technical term for a SAG member who has forfeited their SAG card in order to have the ability to work both union and non-union.

First Refusal – This means that the client has the first right to book you or release you for the date of the first refusal. If you are on first refusal for something and another job wants to put you on first refusal, they get what is called a "second refusal."

Freelancing – When it comes to working with an agent, an actor can either be signed or freelance. When an actor is signed he can work with only that agent, and no others, for the duration of their contract. When an actor is freelance, he is free to work with other agents at the same time.

General – This is not an audition, but rather a general meeting with a casting director to get to know you and be aware of you. This is not an audition for a specific role.

Go See – In the modeling and print world, auditions are often called "go sees." You literally go to a casting director and they see you. Generally go sees are for auditions where the actor or model has nothing to do but be photographed.

Green Screen – When projects on film have backgrounds added to the image, they often shoot in front of a green screen. It's a huge, bright green piece of canvas that is placed behind the main focus of the shoot. During editing, the green background is replaced with a pre-shot or computer-generated background.

Headshot – An 8 x 10 photo, and your most important marketing tool.

Host – Typically you are playing yourself as a host and you facilitate the segments of a show or the interviewing of guests.

Industrial – Films and live productions that are not for the public, but for a smaller, closed-set of viewers. Industrials include training films for companies, live presentations at sales meetings, videos for museums, and the video greetings on an airplane.

Interstitial – Similar to commercials, interstitials occur periodically throughout a program, and often refer to the program itself, or pertain to the program.

Looping – An in-studio technique used to fix dialogue already performed during principal photography by matching voice to picture.

Martini Shot - The last shot in a day of filming. Hearing a director say, "Martini Shot!" means you're almost done.

No Union Jurisdiction – This means that any actor who is non-union can audition.

Non-Union – Jobs that are not governed by SAG, AFTRA or Equity and therefore not obligated to adhere to the union guidelines or rules.

On or About Dates – The approximate dates that an actor will be used on a project. It is important to note that these dates can change.

Per Diem – The amount of money an actor receives to live on for the day if accommodations are not supplied by the production. From the Latin "each day," per diem is a payment to find food and lodging for one day.

Postcarding– Sending postcards to agents, managers, and casting directors to keep them updated on your recent news as well as to invite them to various performances.

Principal – Performer with lines in TV or film. An actor is a principal in a commercial if he speaks, touches the product, does choreography, or is in some way integral to the action of the scene.

Producer – The producer is the head of any production, and usually the one who either financed the piece or procured financing for the piece. Ideally, the producer collaborates with the director, but often the producer deals with all of the non-artistic elements of a play, commercial, film, etc. and leaves the art to the director. The producer is the final say on most decisions (especially if they involve money).

Producer's Session – A callback where not only the casting director is there, but the producer and/or director is present for your audition as well.

Production Contract – Equity designation for a role in a Broadway show, or some other massive production.

Production Coordinator – Person who controls and manages the flow of information between the various aspects of a film project to provide all the required components within the time frame needed. This means that the production coordinator makes sure all necessary equipment and materials are on site at the right times, that staff and crews are in place and have everything they need to work, actors and actresses have their contracts signed and are on site, and all accommodations for the crew and cast are provided

PSA – Public Service Announcement. A PSA is cast and filmed like any other commercial, but there are no residuals.

Reader – In auditions where the actor is asked to prepare sides, there is often a reader in the room assisting the casting director. The reader, usually seated, reads every part of the script that isn't the role the actor is auditioning for. Ideally, the reader is someone to interact with, and play off of, during the audition. Some readers are wonderful. Some are a huge distraction.

Recurring – A role that is on several episodes of a TV show.

Residuals – Actors in taped or filmed mediums often get paid residually, meaning they get a certain amount of money each and every time the image is shown. Residuals are the short name for the money an actor receives for these re-broadcasts.

Scale – The minimum union pay rate agreed to by producers and the unions.

Screen Test – Usually the final step in casting for a large role in a movie or on TV. A screen test is an audition that takes place in front of a camera, often with the potential costars. It's an opportunity for the producers and directors to see the actor in circumstances very close to the actual finished project.

Second Assistant Director – Often there are two or three on a set; they handle checking in the talent, insuring proper paperwork is filed, and distributing script revisions. Actors check in with the 2nd AD upon arrival on the set.

Series Regular – A role that is in most episodes of a TV show.

Sides – Sometimes when an actor auditions, they are asked to prepare a part of the actual script. These are called sides.

Slate – Small chalkboard and clapper device, often

electronic, used to mark and identify shots on film for editing. **Also:** the statement at the beginning of an audition of the actor's name and any statistics that are specifically requested. This is not done in character. For example, "My name is Johnny McActor, and my phone number is 212-555-2345." Not the same as Actors Slate.

Stand-Ins – Extra Performers used as substitutes for featured players, for the purpose of setting lights and rehearsing camera moves; also known as the second team.

Talking Points – These apply to interviews if you are promoting a movie, show etc. Typically you do not want more than three talking points in any interview, so as not to dilute the messaging.

Telephony – A kind of voiceover. Telephony is the recorded voice you hear on automated telephone calls. This can range from, "For English, press one," to a daily recording of dinner specials.

Teleprompter – The device attached to the camera that feeds the actor the words he's supposed to say. It's positioned in a way that makes it appear as if the actor has memorized the lines, and is delivering them directly into the lens.

Theatrical – Describes theatre, TV shows or feature film work, as opposed to commercials. Also known as "legit."

Top of Show/Guest Star – When an actor is credited in the opening credits of a show on television and usually has a key part of that episode's storyline.

Under-5 – A role where the actor has five lines or less. These are common in AFTRA-governed projects, like soaps.

Upgrade – Promotion of an extra performer in a scene to the category of principal performer.

Voiceover – Any voice recording used in a television commercial, radio commercial, film, television show or any media, where the voice and the image are recorded separately.

Waiver – When a non-SAG actor does SAG job, he can either join SAG, or get a waiver (a Taft-Hartley waiver). After three waivers, an actor must join SAG, if he wants to work any more SAG jobs.

Wardrobe Allowance – Maintenance fee paid to on-camera talent for the use (and dry cleaning) of talent's own clothing.

Authors' Bios

Josselyne Herman-Saccio has been a producer for more than 20 years and a personal manager for over a decade. She has successfully managed the careers of actors in film, television, theatre and commercials. She has led transformative educational programs for more than 20 years to more than 50,000 people, programs that are designed to empower and enable people to fulfill on what is important to them and make their dreams come true. She is also the author of *Peace Promises* and *The Promise Effect*.

Guy Olivieri is a working actor (www.GuyOlivieri.com). He's also a producer, a casting director, and a personal marketing coach (www.ActorsWhoMakeMoney.com). He's appeared on *Gossip Girl*, *One Life to Live*, and *Lights Out* (FX), and in over 75 stage productions including playing Mark in the *RENT* National Tour. He's been in dozens of commercials and industrials. He's been on over 1300 auditions and hasn't had a day job in years.

Joss and Guy would like to thank the following people for their support and contribution to *So You Wanna Be a New York Actor?*

Becca Worthington, for her insight and professionalism editing the book.

Wade Dansby 3, for his cover design

Jessica Underwood for her proofreading prowess

Yvette Kojic

Autumn Dornfeld

Valerie David

Sean McCormack

Susan Drumm

Leslie Regal

Emily Gipson

The JHA Team

Emily Kratter

Made in the USA
Charleston, SC
03 March 2013